MY LIFE IN THE CEMETERY:

IT'S NOT AS DEAD AS YOU THINK

My Spiritual Journey through Life and Death

Sandy Doyle

ISBN 979-8-88644-660-9 (Paperback)
ISBN 979-8-88644-661-6 (Digital)

Covenant Books
11661 Hwy 707
Murrells Inlet, SC 29576
www.covenantbooks.com

CONTENTS

PREFACE

In the early 1990s, I started working at a privately owned cemetery during a time when jobs were hard to find. It was a whole different experience from selling insurance, working in a factory, or raising children. The biggest adjustment for me personally was working on commission. I quickly learned to study the cemetery maps to try to find spaces close to loved ones already buried there.

I learned to ask my higher power to send me those to whom I could be of service. Of course, I didn't ever want people to die. I just needed to sell cemetery property and preneed funerals, and I wanted the right people to be guided to me.

I quickly saw the value in preplanning as I watched family members struggle over and over again trying to make decisions for loved ones who had just passed. I witnessed their struggle with not having the money to properly care for their loved ones in death. I saw the guilt people felt at the loss of a parent or child. Hundreds of times, I heard the comment, "I wish I had." I realized that grief could kill a person just like a gun, only a lot slower.

I learned a lot about people. I learned a lot about life. I learned a lot about death.

Every day was different. I never knew who would come in or what experience I'd be going through at any given time. I met people of all ages from different cultures, races, lifestyles, socioeconomic backgrounds. I met some wonderful people, and I also met people who were angry at the world. I was introduced to prejudice I did not know existed. I encountered deep love, and I also met deep hatred.

The job called me into homes with only a dirt floor, homes that were full of rotting trash and untended animals where the smell was so bad, I thought I would vomit. I also entered million-dollar mansions and homes where one could eat off the floor.

I sold cemetery property on the kitchen table, the living room couch, the patio, the hoods of cars. I found that every person who walked through the cemetery office had a story to tell, either about themselves or their loved one, and they told me everything, as if I were their only trusted confidante.

The following is a collection of stories and events gathered from the twelve years I worked in the deathcare industry. Some stories are funny, some sad, some tragic, some hard to believe. Others will make you shake your head in wonder. All the stories are true. All the names and physical descriptions have been changed in order to protect my clients' and their families' privacy.

My prayer is that as you read these stories, you'll realize that we all have unique life experiences and that we can all learn from what others go through on this journey of life and death.

ACKNOWLEDGMENT

In October 2020, I formed a bond with four women after an online Mary Morrissey Dream Building class virtual event. All of us decided we would meet once a week to inspire each other to create a more fulfilling life. I shared with the girls early on that I had a yearning to be a writer but felt that I wasn't capable. I told them I used to work at a cemetery and that I had plenty of stories from all the years I'd spent there.

Sandra Blazynski, who set up our group and is a professional writer, asked me to share a couple of stories with the group the following week, suggesting that doing so would bring me the feeling of being a writer who shares her work. That next week, I read a funny story, a sad story, and a story that had the other women shaking their heads in amazement. They seemed to genuinely love them.

Right after that meeting, Sandra called me. "I want you to hire me to edit your book. I don't want anyone else editing your book."

I hired her. *Wow*, I thought. *I have an editor. This is really happening.*

The next week, I sent Sandra my first twenty stories, most of which were bare bones. Many were only a paragraph or two. Sandra called. "I know that you're interested in writing, so I want you to learn to become a better writer. I can rewrite all your stories, but if I do that, then it's *my* book, not yours."

She combed through each story, sending back prompts for information. Sandra kept asking, "What did the person look like? How were they dressed? Describe their faces, the way they move, their demeanor. How did you feel about this situation? What were you thinking? What did the characters actually say? I want details,

details, details." Sandra took the time to ask me questions to trigger other memories or to pinpoint the main story.

Throughout this process of rewriting, I ended up reliving every story. Some of them made me cry all over again. Some had me laughing out loud. Some had me shaking my head in amazement at human behavior.

Sandra Blazynski—my editor, my writing coach, my champion—stuck with me and encouraged me throughout it all, including a battle with cancer, pneumonia, and two bouts of a sinus infection that put me down for over a month. I stuck with her through the death of her mother, a sister's illness, and two weeks of COVID.

We started working together in February 2021 and completed the manuscript end of June 2022. Through life's ups and downs, Sandra and I completed this compelling book about life and death and, along the way, developed a friendship that will last forever.

Thank you, Sandra. I could not have written this book without you.

THE CEMETERY
KNOWS ALL

The very first family that I served at the cemetery were two young people who had just lost their fifty-year-old father, Jerry Mavis, to a massive heart attack. His eldest son, Zack, was in my office dressed in his army uniform fighting back tears, all the while trying to be brave. Zack's sister April was only sixteen and kept sobbing while whispering, "Why did Daddy have to die? He was supposed to take me out for my birthday tomorrow."

Both Zack and April were in a state of shock. They were Jerry's next of kin, and even though their mother, Sally, was his ex-wife, they were depending on her to help them make some difficult decisions. Zack kept asking, "What would Dad want? What do you think, Mom? April, what do you think?"

April just cried harder.

After much discussion, they all decided they wanted Jerry buried close by his own mother and father. Perusing the map of the Garden of Love, I found two spaces next to Jerry's mother and two spaces below where he would be buried. I explained to the family that those three spaces could be held for sixty days for any family member or friends who might want to purchase them.

After two weeks' time, I phoned Sally to find out how she and the children were doing. She told me they were all still in a state of disbelief and that Zack had gone back to Fort Hood to finish some specialized training.

April wasn't doing well at all. "She cries herself to sleep every night," Sally said. "She was always a daddy's girl, and she always blamed me for the divorce."

I suggested that she might have to get a grief counselor and told her that the grief process is different for everyone and to please keep an eye on how they were all doing. "I can give you a few names and phone numbers for grief counselors if you like," I offered.

"Thank you for your concern," she said. "I already have someone in mind that my sister suggested. And by the way, I've decided to purchase the space next to Jerry. I've loved him since high school, and he was the father of my children. I want to do this for my children."

I told her I would draw up the paperwork, and we set an appointment for her to come by the next morning at 10:00 a.m. to pay for her plot.

Two days after Sally's visit, a dynamic, vibrant-looking lady came into the office, asking to speak with me. "I asked the funeral director at Jerry's funeral whom to contact to get a burial space as close to Jerry as possible, and he gave me your name."

This lady was a knockout. She was wearing a ruby-red tweed suit and a white silk blouse. Her sleek long blond hair framed her model's face. Her lipstick, nails, and shoes all matched her outfit impeccably. She was the picture of perfection, as if she just stepped off the cover of a fashion magazine. She extended her gorgeous hand. "I'm Jennifer," she said. Her face lit up.

"Jerry and I were lovers for over ten years. He was the great love of my life. I want to purchase a space as close to him as possible so I can spend eternity in his presence."

Touched by her devotion to Jerry, I drew up the paperwork to sell her the plot beneath his feet.

About a week after Jennifer's visit, I was sitting at my desk, doing some paperwork when a muscular gentleman strolled through the office doors. He looked like he might have been fifty but an incredibly youthful and fit fifty. He introduced himself as Rich and asked if we could talk privately. I showed him into the arrangement room and asked how I could help him. "Jerry and I shared a special relationship for the last twenty years," he started. "Physically, spiritually, emotionally. We were soul mates. I know that he would want me as close to him as possible, even in death. Do you have a space as close to him as I can get?"

Stunned at this new development and wondering what could possibly happen next, I proceeded to sell Rich the space next to Jennifer, Jerry's girlfriend, at the foot of Sally, Jerry's ex-wife.

Throughout all these uncanny proceedings, I kept telling myself, "It's not my place to judge. It's not my place to judge." Then the thought crossed my mind: *No wonder Jerry had a heart attack!* And wasn't it fitting that he found himself buried in the Garden of Love.

Jerry's family will probably never know Jerry's secrets, but the cemetery knows all.

A LIVING RAY OF LIGHT

On a gray and frigid winter morning in mid-January, my coworker Colman walked into the office after witnessing a burial. His face was glowing, and he was smiling from ear to ear. "Well," he said, "I planted another one for the good Lord today!"

Startled because I'd never heard that expression before or thought of our work in quite that way, I asked Colman to explain what he meant. Colman hung up his coat then walked over to my desk to sit across from me. His face was still glowing and his smile still wide. "Let me tell you a little story," he began. "I wasn't always like this. Over fifty years ago, I met the love of my life. I thought she was the most beautiful woman in the world, and I still do believe that she is. My wife, Lou, has more love and grace in the palm of her hand than I do in my whole body."

I nodded, wondering where this was going.

"We married and had a son, William. I had a good-paying job. Life was perfect, or so I thought. Then one night, Lou, at age forty, had a crippling heart attack. Her heart was damaged to the point that only one third of it was still functioning. The doctor said she would be lucky to live six months."

I was riveted. Up until right now, I really didn't know much of anything about Colman or his life.

"My whole world fell apart," he continued. "I couldn't figure out how I was going to live without her and how I could keep working while raising our son.

"While visiting her in the hospital one morning, I shared my concerns. 'Lou,' said, snatching up my hand in hers, 'honey, you gotta have *faith*!'

"I took her home from the hospital that same afternoon and she rested. The next morning, she was up at 5:00 a.m., reading Holy Scripture and writing things down. This went on for over two weeks.

"'Lou, darling,' I asked on morning three, 'why do you keep getting up so early? You need your rest.'

"'Don't worry about me, honey,' she smiled her beautiful Lou-smile. 'I'm resting with the Word of the Lord.'

"It went on like that, day after day," he continued. "She'd read the Scripture, and everything that had to do with healing, she'd write down. She told me that she speaks God's words back to him ten times every night before bed and another ten times in the morning until God's words get deep into her soul."

I was fascinated now, wondering where all this was going to end up.

"When I took her back to see her cardiologist two weeks later, he said, 'She's no better, but she's no worse either. Just keep doing whatever you're doing.'"

I smiled at Colman, pretty sure that this story was going to have a happy ending.

"That was twenty-four years ago," Colman laughed, "and Lou still refuses to go back to the doctor. She always says, 'When my time comes, just plant me for the good Lord because all is well!'"

I was right about the happy ending.

"I became a minister after that," Colman said. "I try to teach people that God is bigger than anything they're facing. I live with a miracle, and I never forget that. Every day that I do this job, I pray for the souls buried here and their loved ones left behind. I view this job as a ministry, and as long as I'm able, I'll keep planting the good Lord's people."

I was truly touched by the way Colman viewed his job at the cemetery and learned an important lesson from him that day.

The next morning, and every morning thereafter, for as long as I worked at the cemetery, when I pulled through the cemetery gates, I said a quick prayer for all the deceased as well as the loved ones they left behind. Now my work had a whole other dimension, and I started to see it as a calling.

CEMETERY GIGGLES

An exuberant-looking man in his seventies walked into the cemetery office one beautiful summer day. He had a golden tan and gray hair showing at his temples. It didn't take me long to find out that everything was fun for him, even buying his cemetery plot. "My name is Tim Hampton, and *you* are the lucky person who's going to help me pick out my eternal resting place today," he smiled.

I laughed and invited him to take a seat. "Is there any certain area of the cemetery you prefer?"

"Some place *fun*!" he nearly shouted.

"Do you have relatives buried here?" I asked.

"I sure do," he smiled. "My parents are here, a brother, and lots of cousins."

"Would you like me to find a space close to one of them?" I asked.

"No," he smirked. "Just put me as close to the highway as you can get me. That way, I can wave at the drivers as they go by, then I'll always be having fun!"

I laughed and said, "Can you imagine all the car wrecks that'll take place when drivers think they see someone waving at them from the grave?"

"I won't be bored, that's for sure!" he chuckled, and that's the main thing."

It is life after *life* after all.

AS IN LIFE, SO IN DEATH

Part of my job at the cemetery was to lead the cars in the funeral procession either to the chapel or to the burial space as they passed through the gates of the cemetery. I was to stay with the casket until it was in the vault and the vault was sealed.

On a windy, dreary day in late October, I led a hearse and only one car into the cemetery. Since the obituary had listed three children, six grandchildren, and two brothers all living in the area, I found this strange. As well, the deceased had worked full time at a local factory for over twenty years, and the church she attended was also mentioned in her obituary.

While the funeral director was unloading five funeral bouquets, he asked me to call the grounds crew for help with unloading the casket onto the church truck because there were no pallbearers. I radioed the grounds crew. Four of the men came out and loaded the casket onto the church truck then helped wheel the casket to the front of the chapel.

There were four people at the committal service. The minister, the funeral director, I, and a bent-over lady with a cane. After the final prayer, the minister and funeral director headed right out. After a few minutes, I approached the lady, who continued sitting and staring at the pale-green casket with the silver handles and white roses on top. "Are you all right?" I asked.

"Yes," she replied. "I was just thinking about how unforgiving and judgmental people can be. About five years ago, my neighbor Linda finally kicked her husband out after taking forty-five years of his extreme verbal abuse and cruelty."

She had my full attention.

"He went around telling the family that she cheated on him and had threatened to kill him if he didn't get out. Her family believed *him,* and they never forgave her. From that moment on, they all refused to speak to her. Linda became extremely bitter and didn't have a good word to say to anyone after that. I believe she died of loneliness and a broken heart."

As I walked this kindhearted lady to her car, she asked, "Do you think there's such a thing as karma?"

"I don't know," I said.

"Me neither," she said, "but I hope so because I think it would be fitting in this case."

I watched her drive away then went over to witness the lowering of Linda's casket into the vault, praying that she find peace and love everlasting on the other side.

AS CLOSE TO HEAVEN
AS HE CAN GET

On a glorious spring day, I was sitting in the cemetery office with nothing going on, so I thought a walk in the sunshine would be a great idea. As I was telling the girls in the back office where I was going, a despondent-looking sixtyish man walked through the cemetery door. His shoulders were hunched, and he had the saddest gray eyes I had ever seen. Oddly, at the same time, they looked so cold and hard. I thought I was looking at steel. I shivered as I asked him how I could help.

He introduced himself as Herman, and he said he wanted to purchase a mausoleum crypt for himself. "We have a few available on the outside walls but nothing on the inside," I responded.

"No problem," he said. "If you have something at the very top of the building, I'll take it."

I invited him to take a seat in the inner office while I went off to retrieve the mausoleum maps. When I returned, I found Herman staring out the office window with a look of empty hopelessness. "Herman," I said softly, and when he turned to look at me, my heart broke because there was not an ember of light in him, only darkness.

After showing him the map of what was available on the north and south sides of the mausoleum building, Herman replied dully, "Just put me at the very top of the north side of the building because that's as close to heaven as I will ever get."

While I wrote up the paperwork, Herman never said another word. He continued staring out the window, barely there. I gave him the total cost and asked for his name, address, and phone number. Herman pulled his driver's license out of his brown leather wallet and

9

then proceeded to count out six thousand dollars in hundred-dollar bills. I gave him back his driver's license, his receipt, and a copy of his paperwork and informed him that he would receive a deed in the mail in about a month. He nodded bleakly and walked out the door.

After Herman left, I felt a heaviness and gloom consume me, so I went for my walk in the sunshine to burn it off and to fill myself with the promise of spring. I knew I would never know why Herman believed that the top seventh row of the mausoleum would be as close to heaven as he would ever get. It's probably better that I didn't.

FAMILY SECRETS

An anxious-looking woman came through the cemetery doors dressed in a pale-blue linen suit. Her hair was styled in pristine white waves. She was trembling as she asked me if she could buy a cemetery space for her son Ben. "Ben works all the time, and he never has time for a personal life! Plus, he's been so different since his divorce, and I'm worried that something is very wrong," she sobbed, tears running down her cheeks. "He refuses to talk to me about what's going on. I feel like I need to be prepared for the worst."

I took in a deep breath. As a mother myself, I understood her terror. "Please take a seat and I'll be back in a few minutes," I said. I went off to check the cemetery map and found a single space directly above her space in the next row, close to a big old oak tree.

Her mood lifted for a moment. "I love the location, and I know Ben will be thrilled to be by that old oak tree." She paid cash for the space and thanked me. "This is a load off my mind," she replied gratefully as she walked out the door.

A week later, I received a call from Ben. "My mother told me she purchased a burial space for me close to her own," he said.

"That's correct," I said. "The deed has been made out in your name."

"Might there be another space right next to mine?" he asked. "Because I need two spaces together."

I checked the map. "I'm sorry, but I don't see two spaces together in that whole garden."

"*Please,*" he pleaded. "Please keep looking to find two spaces together. I need one for me and one for my partner."

I invited him to come out the next day, and together, we would search for two spaces as close to his mother as we could find. "We can even tour the cemetery grounds if you like," I offered. We set our meeting for four the next afternoon, a Wednesday.

At around 3:00 p.m. that day, I gathered up the paperwork and three different maps of the gardens close to Ben's mother. I had just opened the office windows to let in some fresh spring air when I noticed a car pulling into the driveway with two men inside.

I went to the cemetery office door to greet them. They were walking toward the door, holding hands. One gentleman was older with gray at his temples and a strikingly handsome face with chiseled features. The other was equally appealing with his blond wavy hair, sparkly big blue eyes, and a face glowing with pure perfection. The older gentleman extended his hand. "I'm Ben, and this is my husband, Al."

I invited them in to take a seat and brought out the map of the Garden of Devotion, where Ben's mother's space was located. I pointed out the space she had bought for him and showed him that there wasn't another space available anywhere near that space.

"Wow!" Ben said. "You weren't lying. This garden looks about ninety-five percent full."

"Yes," I replied. "This is our oldest and most popular garden. I think it's because of the beauty of the old trees there."

"Is there anything across the road from Mom?" Ben asked.

I retrieved the map of the Garden of Peace. There, across the road from his mother, were indeed two empty spaces. "We'll take them!" exclaimed Ben. "You won't call and tell her, will you?" he added, worriedly.

"No," I replied. "I won't call and tell her, but I can't promise you that if there's a burial there, she won't be in here demanding answers."

"I understand," Ben said.

Then he asked Al. "Is it okay if we just buy the two spaces and leave the one by Mom vacant?"

Al responded, "Sure, hon. We never know if we might need an extra burial space."

Ben looked at me and said, "My mom is of a different generation, and some things she just, wouldn't understand," he explained. "This is the right thing to do. Write up the contract."

LOVE ON THE RUN

We who worked at the cemetery could never guess what all might occur on a day-to-day basis. Over a couple of weeks' time, the staff had noticed a few teenagers hanging around the cemetery gardens every evening between five and six o'clock, right about the time we were all going home for the day. In everyone's mind was the question as to why teenagers would want to spend their evenings at the cemetery.

Rita, one of the office girls, was the most negative person I had ever met. Rita was short and plump with wire-rimmed grandma glasses resting on the middle of her nose. If anyone said, "It's a beautiful day," Rita said, "Yes, but it'll probably start raining any minute now."

Rita was convinced that these teenagers were up to no good. "You watch," she warned. "One morning, we'll come in and there'll be paint splashed all over the buildings. Maybe even on the graves."

We rolled our eyes at her, but she didn't let up. "They're probably trying to figure out how they can get the bronze markers dug up and haul them away so they can sell them for scrap metal."

"Oh, come on, Rita," I said.

"No, *you* come on," she protested. "These kids'll make a fortune, and the cemetery will lose money. If the cemetery loses money, we'll lose our jobs. How am I going to survive not working with a husband who's too sick to work?"

This went on for weeks, and every day, Rita added a new chapter to her gloom and doom story, including but not limited to the teenagers' painting graffiti on the funeral home walls to burning down the beautiful, covered bridge that connected the funeral home to the cemetery gardens.

One steamy July evening, I had a late appointment at the funeral home. As I got into my car to go home, I thought I saw someone in the covered bridge, so I decided to check things out. When I rounded the curve to enter the charming redwooden structure, I saw four naked butts running for cover under the bridge, leaving their clothes scattered all over the floor of the bridge.

I laughed all the way home and wondered how Rita would have handled this scene. Then I laughed even harder, wondering how many splinters were lodged in these teens' backsides and what excuse they would give their mothers, who would surely be charged with pulling them out.

FLOWERS FOR EVERYONE

Memorial Day weekend was always a big event at the cemetery. Fifty American flags waving in all their splendor adorned the periphery of the grounds, as well as smaller flags printed with the name of every veteran buried there. The grounds crew created special commemorative gardens of red, white, and blue, while visitors brought arrangements of every type and color of plant and flower. The cemetery was truly a beautiful sight to behold.

What might have been a somber holiday always turned out to be joyful, with family members of the deceased walking around the gardens, talking to other family members, laughing, joking, and remembering the loved ones who had passed.

Late in the afternoon on Monday, I was helping a couple find her grandparents' graves when I spotted a glistening silver Cadillac SUV going from garden to garden. I noticed that the occupants were driving all around the cemetery, taking potted flowers and lawn ornaments off various graves and placing them in the trunk of their vehicle.

My first thought was that they were stealing flowers off dead people's graves and wondered how anyone could stoop so low. The more I thought about it, the angrier I got. I was working on getting my feelings under control when I spotted the SUV driving into yet another garden, this time stopping at a grave to haul off a large statue of Jesus.

My emotions went through the roof! They actually had a dolly with a lift on it to help carry the statue to the SUV. Were these people professional thieves? I didn't know, but I was going to confront them.

I handed my card over to the couple I was helping and jumped into my car to head over to the thieves. I pulled up behind the SUV, stopping about two inches from its bumper. There I encountered two robust and beefy women. One of them was wearing rings on every finger, gaudy earrings, and four cheap necklaces draped around her neck. Her piercing eyes screamed, "You better not get too close." The other one was a bleached blond with an overly muscular body. Tattoos of swords, snakes, and dragons covered every inch of her exposed flesh.

I felt a shimmer of fear run through me head to toe. I said to myself, "You better choose your words carefully because these two could purge the whole cemetery if they feel like it."

I got out of my car and smiled excessively big. "How are you both doing today?" I asked, trying hard to conceal my fear. "I'm Sandy, and I work here at the cemetery."

A look of apprehension passed between them. Now it looked like *they* were the scared ones.

I handed them each a business card and smiled again, this time not so big. "I noticed that you were using a dolly to hoist that Jesus statue," I said, looking them both dead in the eye. "That's genius! How did you come up with such a creative idea?"

The lady with all the rings said, "I hurt my back a few years ago trying to lift some heavy flowerpots, so we invested in this dolly with a lift to help protect our backs."

"Wow!" I said, smiling a real smile now. "Do you ladies remove flowers from the graves on a regular basis?"

They looked at each other, squirming. "Yes, we have so many deceased relatives here," said the lady with all the tattoos. "Our parents are buried here. Our grandparents, our aunts, uncles, and cousins are all over this cemetery. That's not even counting our friends who are here."

The lady with the earrings explained. "It's up to us to put flowers on our loved ones' graves, and we take them off early so no one will steal them."

I about lost it. "One can never be too careful," I said, staring them down.

I wished them well and got back into my car, knowing that they were lying, and they knew I knew they were lying. I couldn't prove that they were stealing the flowers, but I wrote down their license plate number and turned it into the office anyway.

KIDS HANDLE DEATH
DIFFERENTLY

After the burial of Martin Payne, a sixty-year-old father and grand-father, his wife, Joan, walked over to ask me how children handled coming out to the cemetery for a visit. "That mostly depends on the children and how they observe family members dealing with the death of a loved one," I said. "The younger ones will just play around and not really pay attention to where they are. The older kids will ask tons of questions about death. Some want an explanation of how the soul lives on."

Joan nodded.

"'Do souls always watch over us?' is a big question for kids. A few will have no questions or response at all. Every child is different, but you need to make sure you answer all their questions. If you don't, they'll think you're hiding something, and they'll get confused."

"When I bring out my four grandchildren, would you mind coming too to help me answer any questions they might have?" Joan asked. "I promised them I'd bring them out here with me if they stayed home with a babysitter today."

I handed her my business card and told her to call me when they were ready.

About two weeks later, Joan called, and we set a time for three that afternoon. At 2:50, I drove to the Garden of Prayer, where Joan's husband was buried, asking for wisdom to answer the questions these children might have. At three sharp, Joan pulled up behind my car, and four children scrambled out of her car. One little redheaded girl of about seven started running around and doing flips. She was laughing, thoroughly enjoying the freedom of lots of soft green grass.

Another little girl of about four with blond curls clung to Joan. The two boys, about nine and ten, were in deep conversation while looking all around the cemetery. I introduced myself to the children, explained that I worked at the cemetery, and told them that I would try to answer any questions they might have. The older boy asked, "How many people are buried here?"

"Over nine thousand," I replied. "We bury around four hundred people a year. The cemetery opened in the 1950s."

"Is there anyone famous buried here?" he asked with anticipation.

"We have policemen, firemen, doctors, lawyers, two ex-mayors, and an Indian chief, but I can't think of any celebrities," I smiled.

Right about then, the little redhead stopped running around long enough to ask me if any kids were buried here at the cemetery. "Yes," I explained. "We have a few children that got really sick and died, and their parents had them buried here, knowing that one day, when they passed away, they'd be buried next to their child."

The four-year-old piped up, "Grandpa now lives where they have different-colored ice cream cones! Grandpa loves ice cream, so I know grandpa is happy!"

Joan nodded her head and smiled. I bet Grandpa was there smiling down too.

MISTAKEN IDENTITY

One overcast Thursday after lunch, I was thinking about how badly I needed a massage. Most afternoons lately had been pretty boring, and I was dreading another day of it. I was lost in the reverie of melting away on the massage table when just then, a robust-looking lady walked through the doors looking like she could whip the world with me in it. I was intimidated, to say the least.

She didn't bother saying hello. "I want to pick out and pay for all my final expenses," she said gruffly.

I asked for her full name, date of birth, and husband's name.

While I was entering her information in the computer, it showed that she had died three years before. I thought I had lost my mind. I checked the information in the computer again and again and again. Yep, this lady was indeed dead.

I excused myself to go to the back office to pull the paper file. Just like the computer, the paper file showed that she had died three years earlier—on her birthday.

I then searched the microfilm, which we always keep as a backup for all clients, alive and deceased. Sure enough, it, too, said that she had died three years earlier. Did I slip over into the twilight zone or what? Boy, did I wish I were on that massage table instead of dealing with this.

Hesitantly, I walked back into the arrangement office. "I don't know how to tell you this, Mrs. Jones, but all our records indicate that you died three years ago on your birthday."

She puffed up her chest and turned red. "Obviously, that's a lie! You can see that I'm here—flesh and bone, blood and tears. Maybe you've lost your mind."

I wasn't about to tell her that I actually was considering the possibility. "Anne L. Jones," I read out loud. Husband: David T. Jones, born July 1, 1960. Address: 111 County Road 200."

"That is not me!" she yelled. "My husband is David *I.* Jones, and we live at 111 E. Main St."

I took in a deep breath, and she calmed down pretty much immediately.

"I know who that is," she said. "I didn't realize she had passed. We have the same name and the same birth date, and our husbands have the same name, except for the middle name."

"Good Lord, what a coincidence," I said.

"I met her in the hospital. We shared a room when our first kids were born. I thought it was a freaky coincidence then, but to know we'll be spending eternity together is unbelievable."

I looked in the computer again and found Mrs. Jones listed on her husband's file. I proceeded to write up the paperwork. She signed the papers, wrote me out a check, and grumbled as she walked out the door. I wasn't about to tell her they both would be buried in the Masonic Garden.

After she left, I was drained from all the weirdness. I called immediately to set an appointment for a massage within the hour. I needed it, and the cemetery knew after that encounter that Mrs. Jones needed one too.

WATCH OUT FOR MY FEET

It was the dead of winter in January, about as bleak and gloomy as it gets. I was enjoying a hot chocolate at my desk after lunch when a couple as different as night and day—not only in appearance but in feelings and attitude—walked in. The gentleman was well over six feet tall and as thin as a rail. "Ma'am, I'm so glad to meet you. My name is Burt. This here is my wife, Genevieve."

"Burt, I can introduce myself," Genevieve replied with a nasty tone. She turned to me. "My name is Genevieve Dalton, and we've come here to buy cemetery spaces. We don't want anything else, just cemetery spaces!" Genevieve was maybe four feet tall and as wide as she was tall. Her big brown eyes matched her short curly hair. The permanent frown on her face seemed to say, "Don't cross me."

I led them into the inner office and showed them a big map of the cemetery. Genevieve spoke up. "I want to be in the Garden of Love. That's where my family is buried, and that's where I want to be."

Burt countered, "No, we should be in the Garden of Miracles because our whole life has been a miracle, and that garden is the most beautiful of all the gardens here."

Genevieve retorted, "No, I want to be close to my family."

Burt shot back. "It's a *miracle* that our marriage has lasted over thirty years. That's where we should be."

Genevieve burst into shouting. "Why do you always have to disagree with me on everything? I want to be buried in the garden of love, and you can be buried in the garden of miracles!"

Burt blasted back, "You must be crazy if you think we're not going to be buried together after all we've been through in life with each other. We *will* be together in the afterlife!"

While Genevieve and Burt were glaring at each other, I was trying to figure out what to say to settle this. Finally, after what seemed like an eternity of silence, Genevieve blurted, "I don't care where you put me. Just don't put me by the road. I don't want people driving over my feet."

Burt busted out laughing. "Put us in the middle of the Garden of Love. I don't want anyone driving over my wife's beautiful feet."

I sold them two spaces right in the very middle of the Garden of Love.

STILL LOTS OF
LIVING TO DO

On a quiet, sunny Saturday, a royal blue motorcycle pulled into the cemetery parking lot. Within moments, a stout gentleman dressed in black leather pants and jacket rolled through the office door. A royal blue bandanna kept his long silver curls out of his face. His black knee-high motorcycle boots made him look even shorter than he already was. He was quite a sight to behold.

"Hi cutie, this is your lucky day!" he blasted, thrusting out his hand. "My name is Troy Stewart, and I'm here to make sure all my final arrangements are taken care of. I believe all I need is my memorial marker. I need to get that taken care of today, and you, little lady, are the privileged one who gets to help me."

Troy was quite the charmer. I walked him into the memorial office so he could check out the displays. He looked over all the displays with great consideration. "Can I get a motorcycle emblem on my marker?" he asked.

I assured him I could do that and that I would try to design it to fit whatever he wanted. "*fan*tastic!" Troy yelled. Then he got quiet and pensive.

After several minutes, he said, "Cutie, this is what I want. I want a light-brown bronze memorial with my name in bold gold letters. Mountains are important to me, so put mountains in the background with a man on a motorcycle. Then put the words, 'Damn, I Wish I was Reading This,' around the vase."

I looked at him to be sure he was serious. When I saw that he was, I chuckled. "I've never put that on a memorial before in my ten years of working here at the cemetery."

24

"Well, I'm glad old Troy is a first for you," he smiled. "I came out today to get this done because my three kids have no idea of who I am or what I want. My wife left us about eleven years ago. I spent my time working, taking care of my children, and making sure they had a good life with lots of laughter. They're all on their own now, so old Troy decided that he's going to see the country on his motorcycle."

"That sounds like a great adventure," I smiled.

"Yep," he chuckled. "I retired, bought a new Harley, sold my house and all the contents, and now old Troy is going to travel, meet new people, and have a hell of a lot of fun. My kids think that I'm crazy or dying 'cause I'm just now telling them."

"It's your life now," I said.

"So, cutie, tell me how much I owe you and I'll give you a check. Old Troy has places to go, people to see, and a whole lot of living to do. No time to waste."

I gave him a price of 1,100 dollars. He handed me a check, bowed to me, and said "Cutie, take care of yourself."

And with that, Old Troy strolled out the door with a spring in his step. I watched him hop onto his royal blue bike on his way to endless adventures in parts unknown.

AND THE GREATEST
THING IS LOVE

One blustery rainy Tuesday in early spring, a gentleman who looked like he might have been in his late fifties walked into the cemetery office hunched forward with his head cast down, a deep sadness emanating from him. He introduced himself as Clyde Smith and told me that he wanted to finalize arrangements for his wife. "Technically, she's my ex-wife," he clarified.

I introduced myself and led him to the inner office.

"My sweetheart was diagnosed with a deteriorating muscular disease about four years ago," he said. "It didn't take long before she couldn't walk across a room or even feed herself."

"That's awful," I said.

He nodded. "She begged me for a divorce. We argued for weeks about it. She was my reason for living, and I didn't want a divorce. Even talking about it was ridiculous. I loved her then, and I love her now. Hell, I loved her the first time I laid eyes on her."

"Why did she want a divorce?" I asked.

Clyde sat wringing his hands and physically shrinking in his seat. "Her medical bills kept rising, and we knew she was going to end up in a nursing home. All those doctors, the tests, the medicines, special foods, and care was going to run in the millions. The little bit of insurance I had would never take care of everything she needed. I wanted her to have the best care possible, so I agreed to the divorce so that Medicaid would take care of all her medical needs."

Over all my years working at the cemetery, I had heard plenty of sad stories. Clyde's was in the top ten. He was full out crying now with tears streaming down his face. "I so hate that I couldn't provide for her the way she deserved," he whispered.

I handed him a box of tissues, and he cleaned off his face and wiped his nose. He sniffled then stood up and dug deep into his pocket, pulling out ninety hundred-dollar bills, laying them on the desk before me. "I've been saving," he said proudly. "I want her put away nice, not in no cardboard box. This I can do for her. Let her have something beautiful."

MUSIC FOR THE SOUL

The cemetery hosted over fifteen different gardens, each with a unique theme and look. All the gardens had lush bushes, blossoming trees, and flowers of endless color and variety. Landscaped with beautiful yellow bushes, flowering dogwood trees, and white and bright-red petunias throughout the garden, the Garden of Hymns was the most popular. Right in the middle of the garden was a twelve-foot-high stone tower with a bell at the very top. Seven days a week, hymns and soft classical music filled the garden from 6:00 a.m. to 6:00 p.m.

An ice storm had hit our area a couple days prior, and even though I had made it to work that day traveling below twenty miles per hour, I knew it was going to be a long day because nobody in their right mind would be out looking for cemetery spaces or anything else.

Around one in the afternoon, a black Chrysler New Yorker pulled into the office parking lot. Out got an older man, limping and walking with a cane. He shoved open the office door. "Why is the music not playing in the cemetery?" he gasped. "I was here yesterday morning—no music. I was here last night—no music. Today—no music. Can you explain why?"

"We've been having some technical problems with the sound system," I explained. "We have a specialist coming out next week to look at it. Hopefully, they can get it fixed or replaced."

"You get that fixed as soon as possible!" he snapped. "I bought spaces as close to the music tower as I could get, and I could go anytime. When I'm laying out here, I want to hear and feel the music. You get that fixed. You hear me?" He glared at me, turned around, and limped back out the door.

THE PRICE YOU PAY

On one of the hottest days in July, two ladies blasted into the cemetery office. The younger one appeared to be in her late fifties. She was dressed in pink shorts and a matching top. The look on her face was pure rage, causing her complexion to be the same color as her outfit. The only thing not pink on her was her silver-blond hair.

The older lady was petite with brown leathery skin, probably from too much time spent in the sun. I could feel the anger oozing out of her too.

The younger one said, "My name is Abby, and this is my mother, Candice Michaels. We're here to finish up all her arrangements, including her funeral."

Mrs. Michaels had a scowl on her face and was shooting daggers at both her daughter and me. I pulled up her file and found that she needed to pay for her vault, the opening and closing of the burial space, and her funeral. "Write up the contract," Abby said sternly.

"I want you to know my daughter is forcing me to do this against my will!" Mrs. Michaels yelled. "I'm protesting this treatment. Abby's being contrary. Do you hear me?"

"Contrary?" Abby yelled back. Her face was no longer pink but a bright red. Her blood pressure had to be over the moon.

Abby looked at me and said, "If your eighty-two-year-old mother were on the roof putting pitch on it in one-hundred-degree weather, I bet you would bring her in here to make her final arrangements, too—provided she lived through it."

Mrs. Michaels piped up, "If my nosy neighbors would mind their own business, you wouldn't have known a thing about it. Those so-called roofers you hired had no clue what they were doing. They sure had no work ethic. As for me, I do what I must. Age is not a factor."

Abby looked at me then at her mother. "We're finished talking, Mom. Just write the lady a check."

DON'T STIFF THE
FUNERAL DIRECTOR

On an unusually warm Saturday afternoon in May, I was waiting for a funeral procession, pondering how sad it was for the family to be burying their mother the day before Mother's Day. When I looked at the clock, I realized that I'd been waiting over two hours. The funeral was scheduled at 11:00 a.m. and it was now after 1:00 p.m.

Knowing that it takes the grounds crew over an hour to complete the burial after the family leaves and that sometimes families will hang around for over thirty minutes after the committal service, I decided that I would call the Malone Funeral Home to get the family's estimated time of arrival. I asked to speak with Mr. Tom Malone.

"This is Tom," he said tersely.

"Tom," I said, "I'm calling from the cemetery, wondering if you have an estimated time that the funeral procession will arrive at our facilities."

"There'll be no funeral today!" he barked. "I'll let you know when," and he hung up the phone.

Because he didn't give me a chance to ask any questions, I was dumbfounded about what could be going on. The funeral had been scheduled for this exact time for four days. In the back of my mind, I kept wondering why anyone would cancel a funeral.

I went into the office and read the obituary for the deceased. She was survived by two sons, two daughters, and many grandchildren. *How strange*, I thought.

Two full weeks went by without a peep from Malone Funeral Home. Then at ten on Monday morning, a phone call came through from Mr. Malone. "I'll be out to your cemetery at twelve noon for the burial of Mrs. Watson," he said. "I'm waiting for the family to get here so they can say their goodbyes, then I'll follow the hearse to the burial site. Someone's coming in now." The phone went click then dead silence.

I radioed the grounds crew to be prepared to inter Mrs. Watson. I checked the paperwork, got a bottle of water, then went to wait for the funeral procession, wondering all the while how big this procession would be since it was two weeks late and why today, of all days, we were having a funeral.

A few minutes before noon, I saw the hearse coming followed by five fairly new-looking cars trailing behind it, all with their headlights and flashers on. As they entered the cemetery, I took them directly to the burial site.

I got out of my car at the same time that the family got out of theirs. Six ladies dressed in their Sunday best went over to stand by the grave. Five stern and stone-faced middle-aged gentlemen walked over to stand close to the hearse.

Mr. Malone started taking bouquets of dead flowers out of the hearse to put on the cemetery's flower stand. The flowers were varying shades of dried brown, all drooping down with no life in them whatsoever. Even the greenery in the bouquets was dead as a doornail. I walked up to Mr. Malone and asked, "Why are we having a burial two weeks late with dead flowers?"

"This family stiffed me for their father's funeral," he snapped. "I wasn't about to handle this one without cash up front. They all promised me that they would have the money the day of the service, but when that day came, all they had was all kinds of excuses. So today, they came in with seven thousand dollars in cash, and today we have a burial, dead flowers and all."

SUDDEN OR SLOW, BOTH TRAGIC

I barely had my coat off that dreary Monday morning when I got an anxious call from a woman who wanted to come in immediately to set up all the arrangements for her husband and herself. Knowing that Mondays were usually terribly busy, I set the appointment for Tuesday morning at ten.

The next day, a despondent-looking Mrs. Tolbert walked through the door. She was dressed in a light-green cashmere coat with matching handbag and shoes. I showed her into the office, and she sat herself down instantly. "I want to purchase a single mausoleum crypt for my husband, John, and two funerals," she said.

I showed her the mausoleum map and she quickly decided on one in the middle of the building.

While doing up the purchase agreement, I asked her about where she herself was planning to be buried. "Across town, at Green Hill," she replied, her eyes misting up. "My first husband, Dan, is buried there, and since we had a daughter together, that's where I'll be."

"I understand," I said.

"Dan died of a massive heart attack about ten years ago," she continued through full tears. "I was in such shock that I don't remember anything—planning the funeral, burying him, or who was even there. Isn't that awful?"

"No," I said, "that seems to happen a lot when a loved one passes unexpectedly. I believe that's a normal reaction. Many people have told me they felt like they were in a foggy daze or as if they were out of their body watching the whole thing."

My comment had an obvious positive effect. Mrs. Tolbert finally allowed herself to sink back into the wingback chair, relieved and relaxed. A few moments went by before she softly said, "After about five years, I married Dan's best friend John. After we married, we flew to Hawaii for a monthlong honeymoon. After we got back to the mainland, we rented a car and traveled to see his brother in Colorado. That night, John had a major stroke and became totally paralyzed. He's been in the nursing home ever since."

Mrs. Tolbert let out a deep sigh. "I really don't know which is worse, the sudden loss of someone you love or watching them die a little more each day."

"Every person is different," I offered, "and how they react in the time of loss is always different as well. The one constant is that loss is always hard."

She nodded her head in agreement. "I have just one daughter, and no matter how I go, she'll be devastated. Today, I'll be doing my darndest to make sure she doesn't have to make these decisions for me at the time of my own death."

AFTERNOON DELIGHT

On many occasions, strange things occurred at the cemetery, and I would shake my head in total bewilderment at the ways of human nature. From the vantage point of my desk, I was able to see cars driving in and out of the cemetery.

One day, I noticed a white convertible pulling in with a young-looking redhead, her hair blowing in the wind. She drove straight to the back of the cemetery where six large mature cedar trees blocked the view from the main road.

I looked at my watch. It said 12:05. I kept waiting to see if she would go around the trees to a grave site, but that didn't happen. Then at 12:10, a bright-red pickup truck drove past the office and went straight back behind the cedar trees as well.

That's strange, I thought, as I proceeded to make some phone calls to help update our files. At 12:50, both the red truck and the white convertible exited the cemetery.

I worked in the office every third day, and every third day, the same scenario took place. The white convertible at 12:05 and the red truck at 12:10 headed straight behind the big lush cedar trees, with both staying there until 12:50. I asked my coworkers if they had noticed these goings-on. They all corroborated that this had been happening every day over three months' time.

One day, I was witnessing a burial, when Jeff, one of the grounds crew, asked me if I had noticed this red truck and white convertible parking behind the big cedar trees in the back around noon every day. The words flew out of my mouth. "They must come out here for an afternoon delight instead of a hamburger and fries." My hand flew over my mouth, and I know my face was beet red. I thought, *Where on earth did those words come from?*

35

Jeff and the guys laughed hard as I tried to explain that I was just listening to that song on the radio. "Either way, you're probably right!" Jeff said, still laughing.

About a month later, on a dark and gloomy day, the white convertible, its top up, drove through the cemetery straight back behind those cedar trees once again. Five minutes later, the red truck pulled in and did the same. This time, I didn't notice either one of the vehicles leaving. I thought I was just busy and didn't see them exit the cemetery.

At 3:30, Jeff radioed me to say that the red truck and the white convertible were still in the back and that he and another coworker were going to check and see if all was well or if they needed help. Ten minutes later, Jeff came into the office, avoiding my eyes. "What's going on?" I asked.

"I just got to see more than I wanted to see," he smiled. "Let's just say that your song 'Afternoon Delight' was right on."

I shook my head in amazement and thought, *If someone thinks their spouse is cheating, they should probably check the cemetery first.*

HE SAID, SHE SAID

Because time has a way of changing people and circumstances, I was doing a project update for a couple who had purchased head-to-head mausoleum crypts over twenty years prior. There were no notes, nor was there any record of contact between the cemetery and the couple over all that time.

I called the phone number that was on the original paperwork. Surprisingly, Mr. Montague answered. He informed me that he and his ex-wife had divorced over fifteen years ago and that he had remarried. "Who was awarded the cemetery property in the divorce?" I asked.

"The cemetery property was never discussed," Mr. Montague responded. "I never even gave it a thought. I just wanted everything over with."

"Will your current wife be buried with you?" I asked.

"No, she'll be buried near her parents in another cemetery," he said.

"Do you plan on using this mausoleum crypt?" I asked.

"Yes," he said sternly. "I bought it and worked hard to pay it off. I will definitely be entombed there."

I asked for his ex-wife's phone number and told Mr. Montague that I would call her and try to get the mausoleum crypt in his name solely. "Good luck," he said. She's not a very agreeable person."

I proceeded to call the ex-Mrs. Montague. "Do you intend to use this mausoleum crypt, or have you made other arrangements?"

"Yes," she answered with great bitterness in her voice. "I'll be using it. I bought and paid for it. If it wasn't for me, he wouldn't have had anything."

I rolled my eyes and said, "Your ex-husband just told me the exact same thing."

"That's okay," she sneered. "He couldn't get along with me in life, so now he has all of eternity to give it another shot."

I hung up the phone, shaking my head, realizing that divorce doesn't necessarily signal the end of a relationship.

HE ATE HIS HEART OUT

On a hot and sticky July afternoon, three people walked into the cemetery office, introducing themselves as Mr. Davenport's children Bill, Will, and Jill. "Jill is the baby, and Will and I are twins, but I'm the oldest and smartest," Bill laughed.

Bill's jovial mood quickly turned sad. "Our dad passed away last night from congestive heart failure. He told us that he already paid for all his expenses but that we'd have to sign some papers, giving you permission to open and close his grave."

I pulled Mr. Davenport's file and discovered that he had paid for all his final expenses when his wife died five years prior. Bill signed the necessary papers, and right after, he and his siblings left to complete their business at the funeral home.

About two hours later, the Knapp Funeral Homes called to inform me that they had had to use an oversize casket to accommodate Mr. Davenport's girth. This meant that I would need to order an oversize vault. I immediately got on the phone to the grounds crew to inform them of the new situation regarding Mr. Davenport.

I subsequently called the company that supplied us with oversize vaults and then placed the order with the heavy equipment crew that would haul over the equipment required to install the 2,500-pound concrete vault.

I was sitting at my desk staring at the phone, dreading and delaying the call to the Davenport children, when a call came in from Jim, the grounds crew foreman. "We have a bigger problem," he said.

I took in a big breath. "Tell me," I said, not really wanting to know.

"The oversized vault won't fit in Mr. Davenport's grave space," he started. "There are burials on both sides of his space. His new vault will take up one and a half spaces. We're going to have to bury him somewhere else."

"Oh, Jim are you sure?" I asked, silently hoping there had been a mistake but knowing full well that Jim always had the measurements down to a science.

"I checked it three times," was his response.

Dazed, I decided to call the funeral home to see if maybe a regular-size casket could work anyway. "No," I was told. "Mr. Davenport will be using every bit of his oversized casket because of his weight, height, and the broadness of his shoulders."

Feeling frustrated and defeated, I called the children to invite them back over to the cemetery. "We're having some issues with the vault, and I need to go over the situation with you in person," I said.

A short while later, Bill, Will, and Jill were seated before me in the inner office. I took in a deep breath and explained about the oversize vault, the special equipment it was going to require to set it into the burial space, plus the extra cost all this would entail. Like a choir, all three spoke in unison. "No problem."

Boy, that was easy, I thought. Still, I had to forge ahead. "I'm sorry to say that that's not the only problem we have. The extrasize vault won't fit in your father's burial space. His vault requires almost two burial spaces, and there are presently burials located on each side of his burial space, one being your mother."

Bill, Will, and Jill looked at each other, seeming somewhat confused.

"This means you'll have to pick out another two spaces for your dad's burial, and if you want your mother buried next to your father, we'll have to disinter her then move her next to your dad. Then we'll remove their memorial and put it in their new location."

Jill was the first to speak. "What do you mean by disinterring our mom?" she said anxiously.

I was really starting to hate this conversation. It was painful for me because I knew how painful it was for the family to have to take all this in.

"Disinterment means that we'll open the grave and bring up the vault that houses the casket. Then we'll relocate everything to the new grave space."

Jill burst out crying, "We can't do that to Mom!" She looked around at her siblings. "How can we do that to Mom? That just doesn't seem right."

Will spoke up forcefully, "Mom and Dad have to be together!"

Bill was the last to speak. "After Mom died, Dad sat in his recliner, and the only thing he did all day was watch TV—and eat and eat and eat and eat," he explained with deep sorrow. He ate non-stop. He did nothing *but* eat." Bill heaved out a deep sigh. "He paid someone to come in and clean and cook for him. And every single night of the week, he had pizza delivered to the house."

Bill's eyes filled with tears. "Dad gained close to three hundred pounds. The reality is that Dad died the day we buried Mom."

He looked at his siblings for their corroboration, which they offered with a gentle nod of their heads. "I'll pay the extra expenses."

SIMPLE JOYS

Many was the time over my twelve years in the funeral business that I wondered why things happened in life the way they did. One day, I received a call from a single mother who wanted me to stop by her home with information on cemetery spaces. She requested that I bring along a map of the Garden of Peace because that was where her father was buried.

When I arrived at her quaint white cottage, I noticed endless beautiful rosebushes beautifying the property wherever my eye landed. I was welcomed in by a lady who looked like she had the weight of the world on her shoulders. She introduced herself as Anna before introducing her two sons Paul and Anthony. Paul murmured hello, while Anthony shook my hand. "I'm so relieved you're here," he said. "We need to get this done so Mom doesn't have so much stress."

I was taken back by his comment and really had no idea what was going on. Anna offered me a chair at the kitchen table. "Anthony has a brain tumor," she explained, "and he's very insistent that we try to get him a space as close to his grandpa as we can."

My jaw dropped at the sadness of this situation, and I felt powerless to muster up any helpful words to say to this mother or either of her sons. I pulled out my map of the Garden of Peace and asked for the grandpa's name. Sure enough, there were two spaces available right next to grandpa. "Maybe God has been saving these burial spaces for you," I smiled at Anthony.

Anthony smiled big and said, "I've been praying that there would be a space for me close to grandpa."

In that moment, Paul abruptly got up and left the table. He went to his bedroom and slammed the door. "I'm sorry about that,"

Anna said. "Paul's not adjusting to any of this at all. My dad died a little over two years ago, and both boys were awfully close to him. Now with Anthony, Paul is having a real hard time."

Anthony said, "Paul just doesn't understand that I'm going to be all right. I'll be with grandpa *and* God, but Paul can talk to me anytime because I'll be watching over him and Mom."

I was so filled with emotion at the wisdom and love of this child that I wanted to cry but couldn't. I had no idea how to respond to this beautiful fourteen-year-old boy.

Anthony then asked if he could pick out his own memorial marker. "I know what I want," he said firmly. "I've thought about this, and I want praying hands under my name. Then I'd like roses all around the memorial because me and Grandpa loved planting and caring for roses. Around the vase, I want it to say, 'I am at peace,' 'cause that way, every time Mom comes out to the cemetery, she'll know I'm all right."

I wrote everything down just like he wanted and asked if there was anything else I could help him with. Anthony sat still in deep thought for a few moments. "Do you think that people have food to eat in heaven?"

"No, I don't think so," I said softly, "because we have no need for food after we're gone."

"That's a *shame*!" he laughed. "I will *definitely* miss McDonald's hamburgers and french fries!"

I left Anthony's home that day wishing that there was some miracle I could give this boy who had touched my heart and inspired me so profoundly with his faith and wisdom.

The next morning, while driving to work, I made a quick right turn into the McDonald's parking lot and bought one hundred dollars' worth of McDonald's gift cards.

I stopped by Anthony's house that same afternoon and handed him the gift cards. He beamed all over with joy and said "Thank you! Thank you! Thank you!" while clutching the gift cards to his chest.

I left with my heart full and amazed that such a seemingly small act of kindness could bring so much joy to another person.

NOT CRYING WOLF

On a blustery April afternoon, I met with a son whose fifty-six-year-old father had passed away unexpectedly. "My mother's having a horrible time trying to cope with the death of my father," he confided. He proceeded to pick out a burial space and vault before writing out a check for those items as well as the opening and closing of the burial space. "I'll let my mother get her own space and pick out the memorial for both of them."

Before reaching the door to leave, he turned back and said, "Give her about a month before you contact her, please. As I said, she's having a difficult time."

Everyone who loses a mate has a difficult time with shock and grief, I thought. "I'll mark it on my calendar," I responded.

As promised, I called Mrs. Hayes a month later, and we set a three-o'clock appointment for the next day at the cemetery office. Mrs. Hayes walked into the office wearing nurse's scrubs. She was the most dispirited-looking lady I believe I had ever seen. She looked like life had been sucked right out of her and was trembling as I led her into the office where we housed the memorial displays.

Without incident, she picked out a memorial for both herself and her husband. Everything was fine until I asked her what emblem she would like placed beneath his name. Wringing her hands, Mrs. Hayes burst into tears. "I killed him," she wailed. "I killed my husband. It's my fault he's gone."

She put her head down on my desk, sobbing. "I'm a nurse's aide, for pity's sake! I should have known better. I ignored all the warning signs."

I sat there with my eyes closed for a few moments asking for guidance and wisdom as to what I needed to say. "Why do you think you're responsible for your husband's death?" I asked gently.

Mrs. Hayes raised her head, a heavy veil of tears still streaming down her face. "The week before Dan died, he spilled acid on his arm at work," she stated. "Like I said, I'm a nurse's aide, so I treated his arm initially, and then every day, I retreated it.

"All that week, Dan kept complaining about how bad his arm hurt and that he felt pain going up and down his arm. Because he was always complaining about something, I honestly thought he was talking about the burn on his arm.

"On his last day on earth, Dan said that his arm felt like it was on fire. I told him to stop complaining, that I would set a doctor's appointment for him to be checked out. Off he went to work, and before noon, he had a massive heart attack. He died before they could even get him to the hospital. So you see why it's my fault he died?" she said tearfully.

I gently took her hand and said softly, "I've worked here over ten years and have witnessed lots of burials and funerals. Every death is different, just as every life is different.

Mrs. Hayes's breathing started to normalize.

"You couldn't make his heart beat. You can't make your own heart beat," I offered. "Something higher does that for us. When it's your time to go, your heart will stop beating, and you're out of here. It was Dan's time to go."

She nodded, and I handed her a tissue to dry her eyes. "Put a baseball player on his side of the memorial," she said. "He loved watching and playing baseball."

She got up slowly and murmured a weak thank-you as she walked out the door.

IT'S ALL IN THE QUESTIONS

Late one sunny afternoon, a middle-aged woman named Sarah walked timidly through the door. "I've never been to a cemetery before, and my father just died," she said.

I invited her into the inner office and offered her a seat. When I checked the files for her father's name, I found nothing. "I didn't think you would," she said. "My father refused to talk about dying."

"That happens a lot because parents don't want to upset their children, and children don't want to think about a world that their parents are no longer living in," I reasoned.

"So where do we begin?" she asked.

"Which would you prefer, ground burial or mausoleum entombment?" I questioned.

"I don't know what he would want," she said. "I'm not sure I understand the differences. Can you explain exactly about each one?"

"A vault is put into a dug-out hole," I explained. "The casket is placed in the vault, put in the ground, and then covered up with dirt. A memorial with the person's name and maybe an emblem representing something that person enjoyed in life is placed on the grave site."

She nodded understanding.

"A mausoleum is a space that opens in the back of the mausoleum building," I continued. "The casket is slid in and then sealed into the back of the building. The name is put on the front of the mausoleum with an emblem that says something about that person."

Now that Sarah was fully informed, she took a few moments to ponder her options. "What are you thinking?" I ask.

"I don't know," she shook her head. "I just wish *he* would tell me. I need a sign from *him*. He left me everything, and I want to do what he would've wanted."

I nodded understanding. "If you were choosing for yourself, which would you choose?"

"A mausoleum," she said without hesitating.

"That's your answer then," I said. "We always want for loved ones what we want for ourselves."

She ended up choosing a mausoleum on the outside wall with a veteran's emblem and a masonic emblem.

As Sarah turned to leave, she said softly, "I hope my dad is okay with my decisions."

Two weeks later, I called to find out how she was doing and was happy to hear her sounding lighthearted and relieved. "I want to thank you for helping me make the right decision," she smiled. "After the committal service at the cemetery, my dad's ex-wife Susan asked who had chosen the mausoleum crypt, my father or me. I told her I had because Dad would never talk about dying."

"That's interesting," Susan said. "About two years before our divorce, we went out to the cemetery to look around and got into an argument because your dad wanted a mausoleum and I wanted to be buried in the ground. I know in my heart that your dad guided you with your decision."

Sarah thanked me again before we ended our conversation. I was elated to know that I asked the right questions and that Sarah had gotten her sign.

A GIRL AND HER DIAMONDS ARE NOT SOON PARTED

Mrs. Jude, an octogenarian philanthropist in our community, had passed away gently in the night, leaving behind a daughter and granddaughter. She was a widely known and well-respected member of our community. A highly accomplished woman, Mrs. Jude had started a women's college, supported the arts generously, and could always be counted on to support the numerous charities in our area whenever called upon to do so. She had inherited her money, had invested it wisely, and had shared it generously.

Her funeral was held on a beautiful fall day. Red-, orange-, and bronze-colored leaves softly cascaded to the ground, creating an air of elegance for a most elegant lady. About fifty people had gathered graveside, along with Mrs. Jude's daughter Sylvia and granddaughter April.

The minister had just spoken the final prayer and offered his condolences to the family. April cried softly, whereas Sylvia appeared stone-faced. The crowd took about fifteen minutes to disperse, leaving behind only Sylvia and April.

I called the grounds crew to come and perform the burial, lower the casket into the vault, and seal the vault shut. The two women departed just as the crew had started filling in the grave with dirt.

Five days went by before I received a frantic 9-1-1 call from Steve, the funeral director at McCluskey's. "We're going to have to disinter Mrs. Jude," he lamented. "We can't find the jewelry she was wearing at the funeral."

"Dear God," I said. "This is just awful."

"Mrs. Jude's daughter has informed us that that jewelry was her grandmother's and that it's worth thousands of dollars," he bemoaned. "If we don't come up with it right away, she's threatening to sue the funeral home and tell everyone in town not to use our facility because we stole her mother's jewelry."

I was sorry to see Steve in this distraught state. Not only did I know him to be an honest and caring man, I also knew that McCluskey's prided themselves on the service they provided to grieving families.

"I really thought I had taken off her jewelry before I closed the casket, but I was so busy," Steve said wearily. "We had so many people here, and it seemed that they all needed to talk to me at the same time. I just can't remember for sure."

Two days later, the ground was dug up, the vault unsealed, and the casket brought up to ground level. Steve unclasped the casket lid, and lo and behold, there was Mrs. Jude in her black satin dress still fully bejeweled.

A stunning ruby choker with a stream of diamonds cascading from the center stone glistened in the sunlight. Adorning Mrs. Jude's left wrist was a diamond bracelet with a large ruby in its center. On her ears were the matching earrings.

Steve was so relieved, I thought he was going to break into a happy dance right there at Mrs. Jude's grave. He unclasped all the jewelry and placed it into a black velvet bag before placing the bag into his suitcoat pocket.

Unfortunately, Steve had to pay for the opening and closing of the grave, a small price for the depth of relief he experienced upon the opening of Mrs. Jude's casket and finding her jewelry intact. Sylvia was equally relieved to get back her grandmother's jewelry, and McCluskey's reputation would remain solid.

Mrs. Jude went to her final resting place all dressed up but no longer bejeweled. I hope she wasn't upset about that. After all, diamonds are a girl's best friend.

DRESS REHEARSAL

I called Jack and Sondra Larson to let them know that the memorial they had ordered had come in and that we had already installed it on their burial spaces. "We'll be right over to check it out," Sondra said.

"Stop by the office," I told her. "I'll go out to the space with you to make sure everything is as you like it."

About an hour later, Jack and Sondra pulled into the cemetery parking lot, and I took a seat in the back of their car. Setting next to me were three large bouquets of flowers. One was all red roses with a single white rose in the middle. The next one had a mixture of purple, yellow, and white wildflowers. The third, my favorite, was an arrangement of yellow and red daylilies with white daisies mixed in between.

I figured that they were planning to place these gorgeous flowers on the graves of their loved ones. Instead, they pulled up to their own burial spaces. Jack threw the car into park. Sondra retrieved her camera from the front seat and jumped out while Jack gathered up all three bouquets of flowers.

Sondra got right to work. "First, let me get some pictures of the memorial without flowers." She knelt in front of the memorial and proceeded to take a wide variety of pictures from all angles and distances. Close-ups of their name, *Larson*; Jack's emblems of a man fishing; her emblem of an artist's easel with paint brushes.

"Jack, stand behind the memorial," Sondra directed. *Click, click, click.* "Now look down on it."

Jack did as he was told.

"Now I'm going to try and capture the sunrays beaming down on the bronze and gold," she said enthusiastically. Clickety-clack. "Got it!" she laughed. "Now put the roses in the vase, Jack."

50

She turned to me. "Red roses are my favorite, and white are Jack's." She snapped the roses from all four sides before Jack placed the wildflowers in the vase. Endless clicks ensued, over and over and over. Then Jack put the lilies in the vase, and Sondra proceeded to click away.

"You two are quite the team," I laughed.

"You must think we're crazy," Sondra giggled, "but we have no relatives left. We wanted to see what the memorial would look like all new and decorated."

"That's a novel idea," I smiled.

"After we're gone, we'll never get to see it, and no one will be laying flowers on our graves."

SHE OUTRANKED HIM

Every morning, the local newspaper was delivered to our office. And every morning, our staff combed through the obituary section to see if any of our clients had passed or if any of the families of the newly deceased might be in need of our services.

Sometimes, the obituary didn't state where the burial would take place. In these instances, we waited for the funeral home to call and let us know that someone would be out and to make us aware of their needs. We always microfilmed the deceased's obituary and placed the newsprint copy into the deceased's file.

On a cloudy Thursday morning, I was reading the obituary of one Col. Samuel Zimmerman. Colonel Zimmerman had spent twenty-five years in the air force. Along the way, he had received the Air Force Cross, the Bronze Star, Silver Star Medal, and the Distinguished Flying Cross. Colonel Zimmerman had been stationed in Japan, Germany, and Italy. He was also a photographer who had received many awards for his work. Up until a year before his passing, he had been living in Italy.

Reading through the colonel's history, I thought, *Wow! What a fantastic life he had! The places he saw, the experiences he had, the photos he took of some of the most beautiful places in the world.* Based on Colonel Zimmerman's illustrious life, I anticipated a huge service, with air force planes flying over and a full military funeral with a bugler playing "Taps."

My reverie was interrupted when the phone rang. Brown Funeral Homes was calling to inform me that Colonel Zimmerman's daughter and ex-wife would be out within the hour to make plans for the colonel's cremation burial.

Three hours later, a sturdy-looking woman with a deep frown on her face walked into the office. "My name is Olivia Zimmerman," she stated. "I'm sorry I'm late. I took my daughter home. She's eight months pregnant and exhausted. If you have any questions, though, we can call her."

"Okay," I said. "Would you like to take a seat?"

Mrs. Zimmerman ignored my invitation and barreled on, all business. "You should have Sam's cremains tomorrow morning," she said coldly. "My daughter, her husband, our minister, and a couple of close friends will be here to witness the burial of the cremains."

That's it? I'm thinking.

"I want you to put his cremains at the bottom of my grave space," she ordered. "*My* cremains will be placed at the top."

"Will you be choosing Colonel Zimmerman's memorial?" I inquired.

"No. Just put his name on my memorial," she said. "If the United States military wants to furnish one, that's great because I'm not spending a penny on him."

My understanding of these events was unreal. Why would the family of a twenty-five-year veteran forgo a military funeral—or *any* appreciation for his service to our country, for that matter?

Mrs. Zimmerman, clearly disheartened, continued. "We were stationed in Italy, and Sam came home one day to tell me that he was retiring from the air force. 'I found a nice young Italian girl that loves me,' he tells me. 'She wants to travel around the world with me taking photographs.'"

I was starting to understand her attitude.

"This girl was younger than our own daughter," she said with great bitterness. "Everything was working out just dandy for him. They traveled the world, and he even had some of his photos displayed in museums. But as soon as he was diagnosed with cancer, the young wife left—with all his savings."

Now she was disgusted. "He came home expecting me and the kids to help take care of him, which we did. If there's any money left, that money can go to the kids. As far as I am concerned, if the air force or the young ex-wife want to memorialize him and pay for it, they can have at it. I won't be spending one red cent on his sorry dead ass."

NOBODY'S FOOL

One crisp and colorful October afternoon, an impeccably coiffed lady dressed in a bright royal blue suit, with shoes and handbag to match, sashayed into the cemetery office. "I'd like to purchase a memorial for my late husband, John Helman."

I directed Mrs. Helman toward the area that held our memorial displays and offered her a seat. When I pulled her husband's file, I found that there was only a single space purchased at the time of his death. "Would you like to purchase the space next to your husband?" I asked.

Her response was a terse no. "I'm moving back to Texas in a few months," she said, "and I'll be buried with my parents there."

Together, we perused a variety of bronze memorials before she settled on one with a vine running around its outside edge. "I like this one," she smirked. "Put his name in gold letters and above his name, put, 'Here lies a genius.'"

I looked at her like I thought she was kidding, and I even laughed out loud. She never cracked a smile. I apologized for laughing and said, "I just have never heard of that being written on a memorial before. Can I ask why you want to put 'here lies a genius' on his memorial?"

"My husband had an extremely high IQ," she explained. "The problem with that was that he thought everyone else was stupid. He had an opinion on everyone and everything. And of course, he was *always* right."

Her mood turned surly. "He even thought he was too smart to die," she said bitterly. "Naturally, the doctors were stupid when they told him he didn't have long to live and that he should get his affairs in order." She took a deep breath. "He was so exceptional and brilliant that he didn't bother drawing up a will or finding someone to run his business either."

"I understand," I said.

She wrote the check, tore it out of her checkbook, and handed it over. "I think he should be thankful that I'm smart enough to take care of his affairs, especially his final arrangements."

"Genius and stupidity are kin" were her last words as she walked her perfectly presented self straight out the door.

NEVER JUDGE A BOOK
BY ITS COVER

On an especially busy Monday morning, Mark from Jones Funeral Home called to let me know that Mrs. Petro had passed away late in the night. Mr. and Mrs. Petro had already purchased spaces at our cemetery, so their daughter would be coming out to take care of any and all additional expenses. "Good luck getting any money out of them," Mark said disgustedly. "These people are dirt-poor, so put the vault on their bill. That's less money I'll have to worry about trying to get."

I thought that Mark's hard stance was strange, given that most funeral homes are willing to work with their clients in financially hard and emotional times.

About 3:00 p.m., a lady walks in dressed in jeans, red crewneck sweater, and a jean jacket. She was wearing worn brown embroidered cowboy boots and carrying a purse that matched the boots. She introduced herself as Lydia, Mrs. Petro's daughter. "I'm here to take care of my mother's expenses," she said.

I informed her that what her mother still needed was a vault, vault installation, and opening and closing of the burial space. I also invited her to consider purchasing her father's needs while she was there, along with their memorial. "We can put those things on a monthly payment plan if you like."

"Thank you," Lydia smiled. "I'll take care of everything for both of them right now."

Given Mark's assessment of the Petro family's financial situation, I was somewhat taken aback. "My parents have been ill for over two years," Lydia explained. "I really thought Dad would go first. They loved each other so much that I don't see Dad living long without her."

I didn't doubt her assessment, given that it's a pretty common scenario for one spouse to follow another rather quickly in death.

"My parents came to this country from Italy during the Great Depression and bought the piece of land that they lived on for the rest of their lives. They raised their own food, sold livestock, and raised me there. They were deeply grateful to be able to live in this country. So just let me know how much money you need to take care of all their final expenses."

I totaled everything up. The final bill came out to 3,100 dollars.

Lydia reached into her worn leather purse and counted out thirty, one-hundred-dollar bills and two brand-new fifties and handed them over to me.

Mark sure did misread this situation, I thought as I handed her back a copy of the contract and the receipt.

Lydia smiled and thanked me. Then she said, "I'll pay the funeral home when I get Mom's insurance money. After the way Mr. Jones acted last night, he can wait for his money. I will not take one cent out of Dad's savings to pay him. Let him wait."

SOME DON'T LIKE IT HOT

One bright and sunny spring day, a new client stopped in to take a tour of the cemetery. Mr. Kindle was a stout gentleman with twinkling blue eyes. I could tell he took extraspecial care of himself. "I just turned seventy," he smiled, "so I think I ought to take care of my final resting place since I have no family to handle this for me."

When I invited him into my car to take a drive around the cemetery, Mr. Kindle said, "Let's walk." I was wearing heels and wanted to protest. Instead, I smiled, thinking that if this seventy-year-old man could do it, so could I.

We had walked about halfway around the cemetery when he spotted the grounds crew adding tree limbs to an already huge brush pile in the back of the cemetery. Mr. Kindle stopped. "Are they going to burn that pile?" he asked

"Yes," I said.

"Don't sell me a plot over there. I can't take the heat. I think it would be best if I bought a space over by the water fountain where I can feel the mist of the water gently soothing my body," he said with great seriousness.

I was speechless and couldn't think of a word to say. "Let's go back to the office and pick out a plot as close to the water fountain as we can get," I said finally.

We turned around to start the long trek back to the office. The whole way back, I was thinking about how I would love to put my poor, aching feet in the fountain for the water to soothe them. I was sure my feet would enjoy the soothing spray of water more in that moment that Mr. Kindle's body would after death.

THREE GENERATIONS
OF LOSS

A sunless day in July brought with it the gloomy experience where I was about to witness the burial of a five-day-old infant. As the sheriff's car pulled up to the grave site, a silver car pulled in right behind it. An ebony woman dressed in a purple raincoat with a matching purple-velvet pillbox hat placed herself close to the little white casket. She was daubing her eyes when the minister approached her to offer words of comfort.

I watched in shock as three armed guards dragged a man out of the sheriff's vehicle and up to the casket. The man was a lighter ebony color and had tears overflowing from his big brown eyes. He was wearing an orange prison jumpsuit, his hands cuffed in front of him. He dropped himself to the ground and sobbed uncontrollably. Over and over, he repeated, like a prayer, "I'm so sorry. I love you. You were my son. Why did you have to die?"

The lady in the pillbox hat ran over to comfort him through his deep distress. The guards stopped her en route, commanding her to not go near him. I turned my head away from the scene because it was excruciating painful to witness this level of human suffering.

The minister, a man of around fifty, was dressed in an expensive-looking blue suit with a bright-blue silk tie. His flashy clothing seemed out of place in this particular situation. He started with the Lord's Prayer and then proceeded to talk about how only God knows why these kinds of things happened. He ended with a blessing for the father and grandmother of the baby.

As soon as the minister spoke his final word, the three guards picked up the fellow in the orange jumpsuit and dragged him back to the patrol car, shoving him into the back seat. I felt outrage at the harsh handling of this father, who was so obviously destroyed by grief. *Are we not all God's creatures?* my mind repeated over and over.

The lady in the pillbox hat walked over to me and took my hand in hers. "My name is Essie. I want to thank you for handling all of this for me. As you could see, my son was in no position to take care of anything. He made a mistake, and now he's paying for it."

Tears filled my eyes for this woman's family.

"My grandson's mother fled the state in desperation. She had to have her drugs, and my grandson paid the price with his life," she said tearfully. "I keep thinking that God always knows best, but I would have raised this baby well and loved him." Then she broke down sobbing, squeezed my hand, and ran back to her car.

I stood there by the little white casket, crying softly for the grandmother who would never see her grandson grow, for the mother who could not stay off drugs—even for the sake of her child—and for the father, whose only memory of his days-old son would be a little white casket. I wept for the precious and innocent infant who never stood a chance.

I called the grounds crew to come and complete the burial and headed back to the office to get ready for the next service.

RECIPE FOR A GOOD MARRIAGE

On a late Wednesday afternoon, an elderly couple slowly entered the cemetery office. The gentleman was hunched over his walker. The lady had the most beautiful full head of snow-white hair, and her soft brown eyes seemed full of mischief. "We're Roger and Beth Shreeves, and we're here today to do some prearranging for our new home," the gentleman joked.

"Roger, be quiet," the lady scolded. "You don't want to confuse this nice girl." She smiled at me. "We're here to finalize payment on any remaining expenses we might have."

I invited them into the inner office, where we all took a seat. Turns out, Mr. and Mrs. Shreeves had purchased cemetery spaces over thirty years back. I pulled their file and started going over all that they still needed: vaults, opening and closing costs for their grave spaces, a bronze memorial, and the cost of two funerals if they planned on using our facilities.

While explaining the differences in vaults, Beth looked at Roger to ask which one he preferred. Roger smiled. "Whatever you think is best, my beautiful lady."

Beth picked out two vaults, two openings and closings, and a chapel service for both. I pulled up pictures of our bronze memorials and asked how they wanted their names and birth dates listed. Beth asked Roger loudly what he would prefer. Roger lovingly said, "Whatever you want, my beautiful lady."

Beth chose a memorial using their full dates of birth and death. She decided to put praying hands on each side of their memorial.

When I asked about caskets, Beth turned to Roger and asked him what color he would like. Roger repeated, "Whatever you so desire, my beautiful lady."

I was so charmed by the way Roger talked to Beth that I commented to her on how great it was that Roger talked so lovingly to her.

"Roger talks like that when he wants something or if he's done something to agitate me," she confided in a whisper. "We've been married sixty years. Only the good Lord knows how or why. I won't ever argue or fight with him, but I will get even."

"How does that work?" I inquired, intrigued.

"We'd been married about two weeks when Roger started yelling at me for something. I never said a word. The next day, I starched his drawers, and he settled right down."

I busted out laughing. Roger gave me a quizzical look. Beth laughed too. Beth leaned in closer. With a twinkle in her eyes, she said, "The secret to a long marriage is to starch the drawers. A man does not yell or fight when his drawers are stiff. It settles him right down."

FOREVER A GOLFER

On a dark and frigid day in November, a couple walked into the office to purchase their bronze memorial. The man was short and muscular with a fading suntan on his face. The lady was short and plump with a scowl on hers. "My name is Bernice Markle," she said, "and this is my husband, Bernard. We're here to do up our marker so our kids won't have to make those decisions for us."

I told them I would be glad to help them and escorted them to the monument display room. Bernice looked all around at the different displays, while Bernard sat down to wait for her. After what seemed like twenty minutes, Bernice finally sat down and said, "We want a double-size brown marker with roses trimming the outside edge. We want 'Markle' written in that fancy writing, like over there. I think it's called calligraphy. Put 'Together Forever' around where the flower vase is. I want full dates of our births and deaths. And put praying hands underneath our first names."

Bernard piped up, "I don't want a praying hand on my side. I want the emblem of a golfer."

Bernice responded loudly, "That is the stupidest thing I ever heard of! There's no golfing in heaven!"

Bernard said sternly, "I don't care if there's golfing in heaven or not. I've played golf all my life, and I love it, so I'm having a golfer on my side."

Bernice sneered, "How can you be so ignorant? Everyone knows heaven is about God, not golfers."

Bernard must have been used to this kind of treatment from his wife because he easily turned away from Bernice to look me squarely in the eyes. "You put that golfer emblem on my side. Thank you."

Bernice's face turned bright red. "I don't know if God will forgive you for replacing him with golf."

Once again, Bernard stared me down. "Put the golfer on my side with the words 'I Want Peace.'"

By now, Bernice was fuming. "Put a praying hand on my side with the words 'I Doubt You Get It.'"

DONE

On a cold and frosty October morning, the daughter of a close friend, Susan Williams, walked through the office door looking like a zombie. She was pale, rigid in her walk, and her face was lined with sorrow. "My husband, Ned, hung himself last night in our garage," she said. "I need burial spaces, and I don't know what else. Can you please help me?"

I stepped forward to give her a hug, and she stopped me cold. "I would appreciate it if you saved the hugs for later. I have to get through these next few days before I let myself feel any emotion. I'm so mad right now, I'm afraid of what I might say or do."

I nodded my head in understanding and silently asked for guidance for me and strength for Susan to get through this. We picked out two spaces in the Garden of Peace. "Ned never could find any peace or joy his entire life. I pray he finds it now," she said.

She picked out his vault and told me how to design Ned's memorial. I placed a race car emblem on his side and a rose on hers. She asked me to put 'In Loving Memory' around the vase. She handed me a check for everything and murmured, "Thank you," as she hastily walked out the door.

I went to the visitation the next day and watched in amazement as Susan stood by the casket, comforting her husband's mother, sister, and her nine-year-old niece. She was composed as could be as she continued to support her family, many friends, and coworkers who stood in line to offer their condolences.

The next day at the committal service in the cemetery chapel, Susan was still comforting everyone who came her way. Finally, she called me over. "Please dismiss everyone and have them all go to the church for lunch," she said. "I'm going over to the burial site now."

After doing what she asked, I called the grounds crew to tell them that Susan was headed over to Ned's grave site. As the grounds crew lowered the casket into the vault, she stood as still as a statue. Then she walked over to the foot of her husband's grave and sat down on the cold ground. For a solid ten minutes, she sobbed and screamed, continually asking, "Why?"

When the grounds crew had finished, they turned their heads away and walked back to their truck. Susan quickly stood up and started wiping the voluminous tears and snot from her face. She then brought out a CD player, turned it on, and played Elvis's version of "My Way." The song echoed loudly throughout the cemetery.

When it ended, she pulled out the CD and threw it into the open grave. Right behind the CD was the CD player. Susan tore off her wedding rings and, in a grand finale, threw them in the grave as well. In a loud, angry voice, she screamed, "It's over! I'm done! You did it your way!" Then she ran into my arms like they were shelter from a deadly tornado.

She never uttered a word before breaking out of my arms, running to her car, and leaving the cemetery. The grounds crew returned to close the vault and fill the grave with dirt as they had done countless times before. I don't believe Susan ever came back to the cemetery.

THE PENNY-PINCHING
MILLIONAIRE

Mitch from Cooper Funeral Home called to tell me that a well-known businessman in our area wanted to come out to buy a mausoleum for him and his wife. "They're not sick. They just want to get all their final preparations done so their children won't have to worry about it when they pass. Their status in the community requires complete discretion. They don't want rumors circulating regarding their health."

"I understand," I responded. "Can you give me their names?"

"Just let them introduce themselves when they come out," he said.

About an hour later, a cherry red Lincoln pulled into the cemetery. Out got a beautiful blond woman wearing a black linen suit trimmed in white with black purse and shoes to match. The gentleman was wearing black dress slacks and a blue-checked shirt with a black sport coat.

As they walked through the door, I recognized the gentleman immediately. He owned the biggest car dealership in the state. He was always on TV advertising his cars. Rumor was that people came to his dealership from all over the state because he had the best deals, and no one left without a new car.

I introduced myself, and the gentleman said, "I'm Will Hatfield, and this is my wife, Linda. I think Mitch called you to tell you we're interested in a mausoleum."

"Yes, he did," I said. "Would you like to go outside and take a look at what's available?"

"Sure, I'll drive," he said. "I'm trying to break this new Colt in."

Once I got settled into the back seat, I enjoyed my first experience in a true luxury vehicle. I was surrounded by soft white leather seats that seemed to wrap around me, making me feel like they were custom-made just for me. Tinted windows, my own personal air conditioner, heater, and music system. The carpeting was cherry red, just like the car, and super plush. Way too soon were we at the mausoleum, just as I was thinking, *I really would love to own a car like this.*

I showed them the mausoleum crypts we had available on the outside wall and explained that it was what we called a head-to-head crypt. Whoever died first went in feetfirst, then the next person that passed went in headfirst. We went inside the building where I showed them two mausoleum crypts side by side. Will turned to Linda and said, "I like these. What do you think?"

Linda replied, "I like these a lot."

"Let's do the paperwork," said Will. "Do I get a discount?"

"No," I responded, "we only have twelve mausoleum crypts currently available. They won't be starting construction on new ones for another year, so there are no discounts on any of them."

"The fact is that I usually don't buy anything unless I get a discount," he affirmed.

I didn't respond as I got out of his one-hundred-thousand-dollar car. I led them to the inner office and proceeded to do up the paperwork. "How do you want to pay for this?" I inquired.

"Charge card," he said. "I'm trying to get enough airline and hotel points to pay for our trip to Hawaii next month for our anniversary."

I laughed out loud and said, "Aren't you glad I didn't give you a discount? You might have been short!"

"Good point!" he said laughing. "Makes me feel a lot better about not getting a discount."

I smiled, knowing this gentleman had the means to go to Hawaii every week for the rest of his life if he so chose. Money makes money, and it helps if one is always looking for discounts before spending it.

PAJAMA PARTY

An eighty-five-year-old gentleman named Melbourne Betz had passed away during a warm Monday night, leaving behind one son, a daughter-in-law, and a granddaughter. At about one in the afternoon the following day, all three showed up at the cemetery wearing matching blue-and-black-checked pajamas.

I was stunned. I had seen people at the grocery store wearing their pajamas, which was bad enough, but after working this job for twelve years, even this was a first for me. Trying not to pass any judgment, I thought, *This family is grieving, and they've probably had a rough few days.*

They paid cash for a burial space, vault, and the opening and closing of Mr. Betz's grave. The daughter-in-law told me to contact them in about a month and they would come out and purchase spaces for each of them.

Two days later, about five cars pulled into the cemetery with the hearse, carrying Mr. Betz's remains. I watched, shocked, as I once again witnessed the three family members emerge from the family car wearing black silk pajamas trimmed in red with black buttons. Black flip-flops were worn on their feet, showing off the sparkling bright-red nail polish on the toes of the women. I found myself wondering if there was underwear under those pajamas, and I bit my tongue hard to keep from thinking those thoughts.

A month later, I called the Betz family to inquire if they still wanted burial spaces close to Grandpa and to find out how they were doing. "We're doing good," replied the daughter-in-law. "Just trying to go through all Grandpa's things and trying to find a place for everything. We'll be out around three tomorrow afternoon. We don't get up until after noon."

The next day, I was astonished once again to witness the Betz trio exit their car wearing the same black-and-blue-checked pajamas from the first day, this time with the black flip-flops on their feet. I welcomed them, settled them into the inner office, and brought out the map of the Garden of Devotion, pointing out the three available spaces the next row up from Mr. Betz. They all three looked at each other in agreement, and the daughter-in-law said, "We'll take them."

I asked if they wanted to put the spaces on a payment plan.

"No," came the reply from all three voices at once.

I said, "That will be 2,100 dollars," wondering how they were going to pay for this when they couldn't even afford clothes.

To my surprise, the daughter-in-law opened her neck purse and, from a good-size wad of money, counted out twenty-one one-hundred-dollar bills. "When would you like to finish everything up, like the vaults, openings and closings, and the funerals?" I asked.

The daughter-in-law looked at her husband and daughter to check, and they both shrugged their shoulders. "Call us in three months," she said, "and we'll finish up everything, except our funerals, then."

When I called three months later, they told me they'd be right out. It was snowing so hard that day that driving conditions were treacherous, so I was surprised that they would even consider venturing out on such a day. By the time I heard them stomping through the office door, I already had all the paperwork completed. With their boots, they were wearing bright-blue velvet robes over their pale-blue-striped flannel pajamas.

When I showed them their 2,400-dollar invoice, the daughter-in-law once again reached into her neck purse and pulled out twenty-four one-hundred-dollar bills. They thanked me for everything before stomping back outside into the snow.

I turned in the paperwork and the money. All the way home, I found myself wondering where they got their money and how much money I could save if my whole family would give up clothes and only dressed in pajamas. Maybe if I told them that every day would be like a pajama party, they would agree.

After this episode with the Betz family, I believe the cemetery had finally seen it all.

MONSTER MASH

A lady walked in the office looking like an older version of a flower child. She had flowers planted in the nest of her bleached blond hair, wore peace symbol earrings, and faded blue jeans with flowers painted all over them. Her tank top was of a yellow so bright that it almost hurt my eyes. She introduced herself as Sunshine. I thought the name fit her perfectly.

"My only son passed away last night," she said, obviously devastated. "I meant to have all this taken care of, but I just could never leave him. He had cystic fibrosis, and I wanted to spend as much time with him as I could. It was the fastest twelve years of my life."

Sunshine bought three spaces in the Garden of Peace, one for her son, one for herself, and one for her ex-husband. "I'll probably have to take care of him because he has no one but me," she explained. This cemetery does allow decorations for the holidays, don't they?"

"Yes, we allow decorations starting three days before a holiday and ending the week after the holiday," I explained. "Then the grounds crew removes everything so they can mow."

"Great, my boy loved holidays, decorations, and fun stuff. I will make sure my baby has things that will make him laugh."

Because it was summer, the cemetery was always full of flowers, birdhouses, wind chimes, plaster angels, and stuffed animals. I never thought about Sunshine's comment again until Halloween rolled around.

Three days before Halloween, I walked into the office to find two of the guys from the grounds crew waiting for me. "You need to go out to the Garden of Peace and have a look at the display in the middle of the garden," Jeff, the grounds manager, said. "The money spent, the time spent, the creativity is outstanding to me. I'm not saying anything else. You just have to go see it."

I drove to the Garden of Peace, and the first thing I saw were two large balloons in the shape of ghosts hovering high over the middle of the garden. The balloons were tied to a wheelchair in which sat a skeleton that looked like an actual human skeleton. All around the three spaces was roping tied to six gory-looking red devils holding pitchforks. Eyeballs, smaller ghosts, and witches were all scattered all over the graves. Spooky-looking jack-o'-lanterns encircled the wheelchair. Spider webbing was glommed all over the three spaces. Music from a black box under the wheelchair blasted Michael Jackson's "Thriller" throughout the entire garden.

As soon as I started to get back into my car, Sunshine pulled up. "Isn't this the best Halloween ever?" she said laughing. "I know my baby is smiling, laughing, and is so pleased with all of this!"

I smiled and said, "I bet he has no words to describe all of this. I know he's having a happy Halloween.

PRECIOUS BABY GIRL

The standard practice at our cemetery was to offer the family of a deceased child under two the gift of a burial space, vault, and memorial. Our thinking was that we wanted to ease the family's emotional and financial burden at such a horrific time.

On a late afternoon in August, I received a call from Steve at Brown's Funeral Home, telling me he would be out with the parents who had just lost their one-day-old baby girl. I thought that was a little strange because the funeral staff normally wouldn't come out to the cemetery with their clients to make final burial arrangements.

About an hour later, Steve walked in with a beautiful lady with thick auburn hair, sad brown eyes, and a complexion the color of milk. She was trying to hold onto a man who was three times her size. His deep-blue eyes were bleary, and as he tried to speak to me, his words were slurred, and I couldn't understand a single word.

I showed them into the arrangements office, where this gentleman promptly slunk to the floor. While Steve picked him up and settled him into a chair, I immediately opened the window to let in some fresh air because the smell of alcohol emanating from him was so strong I thought I was going to be sick.

The lady told me her name was Eva and that her husband's name was Jon. Eva picked out a space in our Angel Garden as well as the infant vault. I told her that she could come back anytime and pick out the memorial for the baby. "No!" she insisted, trembling. "I have to do this now because I'll never be allowed to come back here."

I looked at her ashen face, and then I looked over at her husband who was out of it. I asked quietly, "Do you need help?"

"No," she said hesitantly as water filled her eyes. She picked out a little bronze memorial with an angel emblem.

I asked, "What is the baby's name?"

Tears streaming down her face, she sobbed, "Just put 'Precious Baby Girl.'"

After she signed the papers, she tried unsuccessfully to rouse her husband out of the chair before Steve stepped in to pick him up and carry him back to car. Once I knew they were gone, I dropped my head to my desk and cried for all abused women and for a precious baby girl who had truly little chance in life had she lived.

The next day, Steve showed alone, except for the baby girl he'd brought in for burial.

MORE THAN HER SHARE

On a brisk, windy day in November, I happened to look out the cemetery office window to see an older lady trying to get the door open in her car, but the wind kept pushing it closed. I rushed out to hold the car door open for her. She pulled out her cane to help her stand up. I put my arm through hers to help steady her. I led her into the inner cemetery office and helped her into a seat across from my desk. When I inquired as to how I could help her, this frail little lady started sobbing. "My name is Ethel Yates, and I need to make arrangements for my son Don. I have a space for him next to his own son, but I have to pay for everything else."

I went off to pull her file. I found that, thirty-five years ago, she had purchased eight spaces when she buried her husband. Much to my surprise, she had already had four burials. This would be her fifth.

I walked back into the inner office and was stricken by just how frail she looked. Her face was as pale as a sheet of paper, and I imagined that I could easily count all the veins running through her face.

"My grandson is buried just above my husband, and I want Don buried right next to him. This was Don's son, and he just never got over his son's death," she explained.

I nodded.

"Can you please do up Don's memorial also?" she asked. "Make it just like his son's. Don picked it out, so I want to make them alike, except of course for the birth and death date."

As I was telling her that I would take care of everything, I noticed she was trembling uncontrollably. "Is there someone you'd like me to call and come get you?" I asked.

"No, I have no one now," she responded weakly.

"I'd be happy to drive you home," I said.

"Thank you, but no," she said. "I'll be all right. I always am."

She handed me a check, and when she tried getting up out of the chair, she failed totally. I proceeded to help her up, and we slowly walked back to her car. I watched as the car crept out of the cemetery.

I returned to the office and sat down to read her file. Her husband had been shot thirty-five years ago, a son had been killed in a car accident, another son had been shot in a gang fight, a had been grandson killed in a motorcycle accident, and this son had taken his own life.

I handed in the check and paperwork to the office assistant, got my coat, and started walking through the cemetery. Suddenly, I looked up into the heavens and screamed, "Why? Why do some people have so much tragedy in their lives?"

I kept walking until I finally felt the heavens crying teardrops, and I heard the wind whisper. "It is her journey."

SHE TOOK THE
LIE WITH HER

On a beautiful sunny day in late June, a woman walked into the office wearing a bright-yellow sundress. Her black pearl necklace, matching earrings, and silver bracelet created a sharp color contrast that was compelling to the eye. Her yellow-painted toes stood out against her strappy black patent leather sandals. Her presentation was flawless. She could have been fifty, but she looked thirty.

"My name is Valerie," she smiled with perfect teeth. "I'd like to purchase my memorial. I'm headed to Europe for three months, and I want to make sure I have no loose ends before I leave in case something unforeseen happens."

I introduced myself and directed her into the memorial office. Valerie picked out a beautiful bronze memorial and chose to put her name in gold lettering. A cruise ship trimmed in gold was added under her name. "My favorite words in the whole world came from the Beatles's lyrics: 'speaking words of wisdom, let it be.' I want those words around the flower vase."

I smiled. "Yes, that's a beautiful song. Now, would you like to have your date of birth to be written out in full or would you prefer to just have numbers?"

"I don't want either," she said tersely. "I want no dates whatsoever on this memorial. I've worked too hard to look this good and have told people for over twenty years that I was a lot younger than I am. We can't put any dates on this memorial, do you understand? After lying for over twenty years, I'm not about to have people know the truth after I'm dead."

I looked her in the eyes and realized just how serious she was.

"Leave it blank," she ordered. "Let people guess. Some things are better left unknown, and my actual age is one of them. I will take my age to my grave. After all, age is only a number."

She handed me a check, got up, and sashayed out the door.

TOO PROTECTED
OR TOO LOVED

On a hot day in July, a morbidly obese woman trudged through the office doors looking forlorn and lost. I introduced myself and asked how I could help her Although she looked right at me, I don't believe she saw me or heard a word I said. Finally, she groaned, "My husband had a heart attack this morning. "He died in my arms, and I don't know what to do. About two months ago, he said that we needed to go out to the cemetery to pick out our burial spaces, but we never got around to it.

I led her into the arrangements office and gently walked her through the process of picking out spaces, vaults, and chapel service. The longer the process took, the more agitated she became.

When I handed her a copy of the bill, she started shaking. She reached into her purse and handed me her checkbook. "Will you please fill out the check?" she asked. "I've never written a check in my life. Carl always took care of everything. He paid the bills. He bought whatever we needed. He went to the grocery. He took care of the yard. He maintained our house and our car."

She started whimpering, "I told him for years that I would go before him. Carl was my everything. How am I going to live without him?" She laid her head on the desk and bawled uncontrollably.

I closed my eyes and prayed for help for her, asking that I counsel her well, knowing that she probably would barely hear or remember anything I said because of her emotional state.

After what seemed like an eternity, her cries turned to sobs, and her sobs turned to sniffles. I handed her a box of tissues. I gave her a few moments to compose herself before handing back her checkbook, receipt, and a folder. "Inside this folder is a list of forty different decisions that must be made within the next few days. Use it as your guideline."

I then asked her if she had a friend or relative to help her through these next few days. She nodded, and softly whispered, "My sister is coming from Texas tomorrow."

I smiled and handed her another paper. "This outlines the five stages of grief. Keep in mind that the grief process is different for everyone. Read this every week to determine where you are in the grieving process. It takes as long as it takes, from weeks to years. If at any time you feel you need help, get some counseling. There are therapists who specialize in grief therapy.

She grabbed the paper and shoved it into the folder. She left the office that day looking like life had left her too. I don't know whether she ever got counseling, but I had the feeling that she died the same way her husband did, only it took a couple years for her grief to bury her.

HOME STORIES

Many was the time, for a variety of reasons, when I was called to clients' homes to work with them there. The following are their stories.

PLANTED CORN

One day, I took a call from established clients, asking me to stop by for a house call. I had worked with the man and his wife about six months prior finishing up their funeral plans. "What's going on?" I asked.

"My mother and father need to get all their affairs in order," their son Patrick informed me. "My father had a stroke about six weeks ago, and I just found out that they only bought their cemetery plots and that was about forty years ago."

"I understand," I said. "What would you like me to do?"

"Can you please go to my mom's house and get everything that's needed down on paper? I know she has the money to do it, but I don't know if she's willing to part with it right now."

I set the appointment for the next day.

On my way to Bertha and James's home, I passed by fields full of corn. The sun was shining, and I had my radio playing full blast, singing along with it. I thought how blessed I was to be out of the office while working. I pulled into the driveway, noticing the beautiful flowers of every color growing all around the white picket fence.

Sitting on the large white wraparound porch was a white-haired lady, waving at me. I walked up the steps and introduced myself. "Hello, dear, I'm Bertha," she said, giving me the warmest smile I'd ever seen. Bertha was wearing a floral housedress with a bright-yellow apron. "I've fixed us some fresh lemonade. Please come on into the kitchen."

Bertha's kitchen table was covered with a red-checkered tablecloth. In the center of the table sat a vase full of the most fragrant white roses. I took my seat. Bertha handed me my glass of lemonade. "Thank you for coming out," she said, taking her seat. "My eyesight isn't good enough for me to drive anymore. I guess that happens when you turn eighty."

While I took a sip of lemonade, Bertha's mood took a turn for the worse. Tears filled her eyes. "My James had a stroke about six weeks ago," she said, "and now we both must go into assisted living. James will be in the medical part, and I'll have my own apartment. I must sell our home, barns, equipment, and all three hundred acres of our farmland." Bertha put her head down on the table as her tears turned to sobs.

I closed my eyes and asked for guidance as to what to say because I had no words.

When Bertha stopped sobbing, she lifted her head and looked at me. "I'm so sorry for the meltdown, but this is our home. We built this house. We built the barns. We bought the land fifty acres at a time. We've been here sixty-two years! We raised our children here. Now all of it must be sold to take care of our medical bills and our care."

I reached out and placed my hand on hers. "You have every right to be upset. This is a tremendous amount of loss and adjustments for you both to go through."

Bertha dried her eyes and took a sip of lemonade. "Thank you again for being here," she smiled weakly.

I brought out my books on caskets, vaults, and memorials, and we discussed the various ways of designing a funeral. Bertha made her choices. "How much is all this going to cost me?" she asked.

"The vaults, installation of vaults, openings and closings comes to a total of 1,800 dollars. A double bronze memorial will be 1,700 dollars. Two funerals and two wooden caskets will cost you eighteen thousand dollars."

Bertha looked at me like I was crazy. "How much more would it have cost me if I had not purchased our spaces forty years ago?"

"Those exact same spaces today are 1,600 dollars," I said. "You paid two hundred dollars for them forty years ago."

Bertha shook her head over and over, unable to grasp her predicament. "I wish we had planted people instead of corn."

A LITTLE CLARITY
GOES A LONG WAY

Robert Michaels came into the office one Tuesday morning to pay for his brother John's cemetery expenses. John had died from a heart attack a few days prior, leaving Robert as his only surviving relative. After Robert finalized payment, I informed him that I would be calling him in about two weeks to find out how he was doing and to see if he had any questions. Robert shrugged and walked out without saying a word.

Two weeks later, I placed the call. "I'm doing all right," he said flatly. "I'm just mad."

"Why is that?" I asked.

"John didn't have to die," he said. "The doctor told him six weeks ago that he needed stents put in his heart. John ignored the doctor's advice. I guess he thought he wasn't going to die."

"I'm so sorry, Robert," I said. "It must be so hard, knowing that this could have been prevented or not. Maybe your brother felt it was his time to go."

"You might be right, but he could have told me," he said sadly.

I asked if I could come out to his house to share some information with him and his wife about starting some of their prearrangements. "You can come out and leave us some information," he said defiantly, "but I've already told my wife to cremate me. Throw me in the backyard, the trash, whatever she wants to do. There's no reason to spend a bunch of money on burials."

"Is tomorrow early evening about six okay for me to come out?" I asked, ignoring his comments.

The next day near dusk, I pulled into their driveway and was taken by their perfectly landscaped yard with colorful shrubs and flowers everywhere my eyes landed. I was met by a pretty suntanned lady with sun-streaked hair. She introduced herself as Mae, Robert's wife. "Come on into the back yard," she smiled. "I've fixed us some fresh ice tea."

I sat down at the patio table where Robert was already seated. After a few sips of tea, I started my presentation. While Mae asked questions, I noticed John was in another world, paying no attention to a word I was saying.

I gazed out into their gorgeous backyard. The yard was resplendent with beauty, color, lush life. Their heart-shaped pool's waterfall generated a soothing sound. I let out a sigh. "Robert," I said, "I don't blame you for wanting your cremains to be buried here when you pass, maybe over there by the lilies. Maybe Mae could place her cremains amongst the roses. It's obvious she's put a lot of love into her flowers. This is truly an oasis, and I can understand why you would want to spend eternity here."

I continued even though Robert 's face was beet red. "You could offer up your entire yard for the cremains of all your family members, but remember that if there are human remains on a property, it must be recorded with the county office."

Mae looked at Robert dumbfounded. Then she turned to me and stated, "This is something we'll be discussing. Please leave us all the information and we'll be in touch."

I said my goodbyes and wished them well, figuring I'd never hear from them again.

A week later, Mae and Robert walked into the cemetery office, asking for me. Mae said, "We've talked all this over, and after going through everything that we just went through with Robert's brother John, we've decided to get all our prearrangements set up and paid for."

I wrote up the contract up for two spaces; two cremation vaults; a double bronze memorial with their names in gold lettering with an emblem of roses on Mae's side, waterfalls on Robert's; two funeral services; and two wooden caskets used for cremation. The total came to fourteen thousand dollars. They thanked me for helping them to see the value of preplanning.

This was one of those days when nothing major happened, but I went home that night feeling gratified, knowing that I'd done a good job of preventing headaches sometime in Mae and Robert's family's future. All they needed was a little clarity, and I was happy to be the one to provide it for them.

NO FORGIVENESS

Mrs. Crabtree came into the cemetery office one chilly day in late September to make all the cemetery arrangements for her husband, Amos, who had passed the night before. She had a harsh, stern look on her face that went perfectly with the dull-gray suit she was wearing. Her gray eyes matched the suit, and her face had many lines, especially around her mouth. "I want to purchase two spaces, two vaults, two openings and closings, one for my husband and one for me," Mrs. Crabtree said all businesslike.

"Where in the cemetery would you like to be?" I asked.

"It makes no difference as long as he gets in the ground," she said, her eyes narrowing.

I thought I was going to lose my composure. Never in all my time at the cemetery had I ever heard something so cold, and the way she said it made me cringe inside. "Do you want to order the memorial now or wait for later?" I asked.

"Give me two weeks and then call me," she replied and then walked out the door.

Two weeks later, I set an appointment at Mrs. Crabtree's home for the following day. That day, I found myself in a beautiful two-story brick home with flowers outlining the driveway and sidewalk. Mrs. Crabtree greeted me at the door and ushered me into the dining room. No small talk, nothing, just straight business. I showed her a catalog with various types of memorials. She picked out a blue-bronze one, with gold lettering. "Would you like to place emblems above your names?" I offered.

"No, it's not necessary," she said.

"Would you like the words 'Together Forever' encircling the vase, or do you prefer 'In God's Loving Care'?"

"I don't want either," she near spat. "Just leave it plain. We weren't together. He went his way, and I went mine."

I was shocked and was all ready to have her sign the contract when she offered, "When Amos and I married thirty-five years ago, we were happy. We started a business, decided to have two children. We made the decision that I would stay home and raise our children, which I loved with all my heart."

After a thoughtful pause, she continued, "One day, Amos came home, and I was telling him about how much fun the kids had had that day picking out their new puppy. Out of nowhere, Amos exploded. 'Shut up!' he said. 'I don't need to hear about all your trivial stuff. You don't have anything important to say, and I have more pressing things to think about. You can't talk about anything other than those kids.'"

Wow.

"I moved out of the bedroom that night, and I never spoke to him again after that," she said flatly. "About five years ago, Amos had a stroke that left him completely paralyzed. I put him in the nursing home and proceeded to run the business. I never went to the nursing home. I was done. I bet he would have loved for me to talk about trivial stuff then."

Mrs. Crabtree signed the contract and wrote out the check for everything, including the plain-blue memorial that only had their names on it.

I wished her well and left thinking, *Forgiveness does not excuse behavior, but forgiveness prevents others' behavior from destroying your heart.*

That night, I prayed that Mrs. Crabtree find forgiveness for both her husband and for herself.

NO TIME FOR DEATH

The funeral home received a call from the nearby nursing home, informing them that one Mr. McCowan had passed during the night. The nursing home reported that they had contacted his son in another state about his father's death and gave the funeral director the son's name, Thomas McCowan, along with his contact information.

The funeral director tried to contact Thomas throughout the day but got no response. They tried again the next day, leaving several calls and messages. Still no response. On the third day, the funeral director called me to ask if I would try to contact Mr. McCowan's son because he had two funerals to tend to that day. "I know you worked with Mr. McCowan before he went into the nursing home on all his cemetery needs, and the notes say that the son will take care of the funeral."

"Yes, that's correct," I said. "Mr. McCowan told me that his son was a lawyer and that he would take care of everything. He seemed so proud of him."

Late that afternoon, I finally got through to Mr. McCowan's son. "I'm a lawyer," he said, "and I'll be in court for the next two weeks. I don't have time to mess with all this. I won't be there, so just do whatever you think needs to be done and fax me the bill."

We buried Mr. McCowan in an oak casket with a United States Navy emblem stitched into the casket lid. An American flag draped his casket.

A few people from the nursing home came to the funeral. Each one made a comment about what a nice, funny man Mr. McCowan was and how proud he was of his son. An honor guard, the funeral director, and I stood at Mr. McCowan's grave site, listening to the tune "Taps" resonating throughout the cemetery. The honor guard methodically folded the American flag and placed it into a case to be shipped to Mr. McCowan's son.

Over those few days, the United States Navy, the nursing home employees, the funeral director, and I had personally shown more respect for the life that Mr. McCowan had lived than his own son, of whom he was so proud.

LOVE HAS MANY FORMS

One afternoon, I decided to do some follow-up work with families that had lost a loved one within the last month. I always tried to check on the families to make sure they were satisfied with the service we had provided and answer any questions they might have.

My first call was to Viny Jennings who had recently made all the arrangements for her Aunt Lydia. I found myself in a game of twenty questions. Viny wanted to know about vaults, caskets, tombstones, funeral details, and the cost of transporting caskets from our town to Tennessee for burial. I informed her that I would have to check with the funeral home to get the per-mile rate. "I'll call you back with the pricing for everything the first of next week," I told her.

A week later, I called Viny back. She asked me if I could come to her home and share all my information with her husband, Ralph. I set the appointment for the next day at six, right after work.

Upon arriving, I encountered a man who did not want to talk about anything, especially funerals and death. Ralph informed me he was only fifty years old and that when the time came, he planned on going back to Tennessee to be buried in his family cemetery. Viny jumped in forcefully, "*We* need to hear all the information so *we* can be informed. Only God knows about tomorrow."

I proceeded to show them pictures of vaults and informed them that the vaults help protect the ground from sinking. I then showed them pictures of caskets and explained the differences between those made of wood and those made of metal as well as explaining the different gages of metal caskets.

Viny picked out the vault and casket she wanted and asked Ralph if he wanted anything different. "I'm not going to be here, so I don't care," he replied.

Viny ignored Ralph and asked me to total up everything for them both. Two vaults, vault installation, two wooden caskets, two funerals here in our city, and the cost of transporting Ralph's body to Tennessee for burial. "For both of you, the cost will be twenty thousand dollars," I said.

I thought Ralph was going to pass out. "That's ridiculous! There's no way things should cost that much. Break down all those figures for me," he commanded.

I had already been in their home close to two hours and felt drained, but for some reason, I felt this was important for Viny. I showed Ralph my writing pad and proceeded to go over each item: two thousand dollars for two vaults and installations, two thousand dollars for two trips to Tennessee with the funeral director staying with the bodies until they're in the ground, sixteen thousand dollars for two caskets and two funerals. Total: twenty thousand dollars.

Ralph kept shaking his head and staring at the figures. Viny went to another room and came back with the checkbook. Viny handed Ralph the checkbook. "Write her a check. I want this done, and I want it done now."

Obeying Viny's order, Ralph got to the business of writing the check for everything, grumbling under his breath the whole time.

Three months later, Viny died of causes unknown, but I believe she knew she was dying and that she was saving Ralph from having to make all these decisions without her.

HOW WE LIVE AND
HOW WE DIE

In the middle of November, just days before Thanksgiving, I was idling in the office, thinking about how slow business was. People tend to die after the holidays, but before, business is molasses slow. It's as if people fight to hang on long enough to spend one last holiday with their loved ones.

A call came in at noon, and I snatched up the phone. A lady's voice weakly said, "I just got out of the hospital, and I'm dying."

I was taken aback because I had never heard a conversation start with those words. Ina introduced herself and asked me if there was any way I could come to her house because she didn't have the strength to come out to the cemetery. I told her I would be there at ten the next morning.

Driving up to Ina's home, I encountered overgrown weeds taller than me. The house literally looked like it was falling down. The roof had a bright-blue tarp covering up the whole right side of the house, with rocks and bricks holding the tarp in place. Pieces of siding and roofing were scattered all over the yard amongst all the trash.

I approached her front door and the first of three steps. After the first step creaked and cried from the strain of my being on it, I held my breath through steps two and three, hoping to make myself weigh less in order to avoid splintering the steps to smithereens. I knocked and knocked on the dull-gray and peeling paint on the front door, but there was no answer. I walked around to the back door and tried there. Finally, I heard a raspy voice yell at me to come on in.

As I opened the door to go into the garage, I suddenly found myself surrounded by trash and filth of a magnitude I'd never encountered before in life. Old newspapers, used tissues, unrinsed empty tin cans, empty beer bottles lay scattered all over what appeared to be a garage floor. I put my hand on the door handle to go into the house and recoiled at the grime and dirt caked there from ages past. I shut my eyes and prayed. "God, please help me with this. I feel like I'm going to be sick, and this lady needs my services."

Too many smells attacked my nostrils simultaneously once I opened the door to Ina's house: cat litter, cat urine, rotted food, stale beer, filth of unknown origins, and the sweet-and-sour smell of poverty hit me all at once like a ton of bricks. There at the kitchen table sat a worn-out ashen-colored old lady with stringy, greasy gray hair, about fifty pounds overweight. She was wearing a faded and tattered sweatshirt with food stains all over the front with red flannel pajama bottoms.

Ina sat there unmoving, puffing on a cigarette while laboring to breathe. Her oxygen tank was not keeping up with her gasps for breath, and I prayed that the place wouldn't explode. I found myself wondering if Ina had *ever* had a bath, not when was the last time she took one.

I introduced myself, and she rattled back, "Hi, honey. Please sit down." When I took my seat at the kitchen table opposite her, she noticed that I had no room to put down my binder because of all the dirty paper plates, beer bottles, plastic utensils, and cups covering every square inch of that tabletop.

There was encrusted old food still on all the paper plates and stale beer stagnating in greasy bottles. Ina took in a deep, raspy breath, picked up her end of the table, and sent everything flying to the floor. The black cat that had been curled up at her feet darted off to the other room like a shot, while the sound of glass breaking filled the room.

I put my binder on the table and cringed, knowing that the table had not been wiped down in years. I started writing up the contract for her burial space, vault, opening and closing of the grave, and her memorial. I told her the total was 2,600 dollars.

I sat there watching, utterly disgusted, as Ina pulled her filthy sweatshirt up to the level of her shredded yellowing bra and pulled out a wad of cash. She proceeded to count out twenty-six one-hun-dred-dollars bills, laying them one by one on top of my binder. The money was musty and reeked of sweat. I felt nauseated. When she finished, it took all Ina's breath to get the rest of her stash back into her bra.

I proceeded to write up her biographical information and dis-covered that Ina lived in that house with her husband and three grown sons. She was from the hills of Virginia, married at fourteen, and had worked at a factory in town for twenty years. She had no other living relatives.

Ina's rattling breathing had gotten worse since I'd arrived, and she was having a real hard time taking in sufficient oxygen. The last ten minutes I was there, I was terrified that she was going to die on me right then and there.

I got up to leave and wished her all the best. I walked out into the fresh air and took the deepest breath of my life, realizing that the whole time I was there, I was either trying not to breathe at all or was breathing into my winter scarf. I thanked God for fresh air and my ability to breathe it in. I was beside myself, wondering how people could allow themselves to live like that and felt both angry and saddened by it.

When I got home, I walked straight to the shower and scrubbed my body down twice. The stench of Ina's sad dwelling had soaked into my flesh. I threw my clothes into the wash—even my coat and scarf—sterilized my shoes, my purse, my binder. I sprayed the money Ina pulled out of her bra with disinfectant. Then I sat down in my recliner and cried.

Ina passed away the day after Thanksgiving, and I found myself wondering if it was the disease that killed her or her living condi-tions. Maybe it was both.

NEVER JUDGE A BOOK
BY ITS COVER

One day while working in the office, I received a call from a lady who asked me if there was any way I could come to her house and help her pick out a memorial for herself and her deceased husband. The next day, as I was driving over to the address she'd given me, I realized that I was in the very poorest part of town.

Even though the husband had died four years prior, I found myself wondering how this lady would be able to afford a memorial—or anything at all, for that matter. Every house in the neighborhood looked like they were ready to collapse at any moment. All that was needed was one strong gust of wind to come along and demolish every one of them.

I pulled up in front of a blue two-story house with shingles missing on every section of the roof and discarded siding lying on the ground. The wooden planks on the porch shrieked under the pressure of my weight. Big boxes piled high filled the porch space, as if someone was either moving in or out.

I knocked and knocked for at least five minutes. When I finally gave up and started to walk back to my car, the door opened, and an elegant lady dressed in a flowing red gown was standing in the doorway. Her hair was piled on top of her head in a beautiful crown of curls. She wore expensive-looking rings on every finger and a necklace that appeared to be made of top-grade diamonds. Her red lips and nail polish matched her dress perfectly. Astounded at the sight of her, I managed to stammer out my name.

"My name is Lavinia," she smiled with perfect teeth. "Come on into the parlor. We'll be more comfortable there."

I stepped onto a crimson wall-to-wall carpet and sat down where she pointed me to sit on a royal blue Victorian settee. In the middle of the room was a white baby grand piano. My eyes landed on top of the piano, where a large gilded-framed picture of a nice-looking gentleman sat.

"That was my husband, Lorenzo," she offered. "He was such a good man. He pulled me out of the slums and taught me how to be a lady. He bought me this piano and taught me how to play. So now, every morning, I play for him." She went silent, looking out into space for a few minutes.

Lavinia came over and sat down beside me to look at the memorials catalogue I'd brought. She chose a brown bronze one with gold lettering. Above her name would be a piano, and on Lorenzo's side would be a military emblem representing the army. The words "Together Forever" would encircle the vase.

When it came time to settle the bill, I informed her that the cost would be 1,550 dollars. "Would you like to put this on a payment plan?" I asked.

"No, this will be cash," she said as she sashayed over to the piano bench, lifted the top, reached in, and pulled out fifteen one-hundred-dollar bills and one fifty-dollar bill.

When she handed me the money, I must have looked stunned because she chuckled, "Oh, that's out of my rainy-day fund." Then with a sparkle in her eyes, she said. "Every woman needs one, you know. Just don't let anyone know you have one because people will find a reason to take it from you."

NOT READY TO
FACE DEATH

I had set a 2:00-p.m. appointment with Clara Beaty at her home for the following day to bring the deeds for her cemetery property and to go over her next preplanning steps. When I arrived, I found no one at home. While waiting around in my car for fifteen minutes, I noticed the guy next door working in his yard. Every few minutes, he stopped to stare at me.

When it became clear that Clara wasn't coming, I left a note and my card at her front door then headed over to the guy next door to introduce myself and hopefully get a lead. When he realized that I was headed in his direction, he yelled in an angry tone, "What the hell do you want?"

Flabbergasted, I smiled, introduced myself, and told him I was from the cemetery. "Cemetery?" he shrieked. "Oh, *hell no!* I am *not* talking to any of those graveyard people." He threw down his rake and literally ran to his front door. Before he went inside and slammed the door, he looked back at me, shaking his head.

When I got back into my car, I found myself shaking. Then I decided that I had had enough rejection for the day and was going home. On my way home, I found myself reliving that experience, thinking, "I bet his family one day will wish he had talked to a graveyard person."

JACKPOT

Any warm, sunny days made it hard for me and my coworker Bernice to be in the office. While everyone else was outside working in their yards enjoying the sunshine, we were stuck in the office with no appointments and not in the mood to do anything to get them.

After our weekly meeting, we all went out to lunch. We decided to walk the neighborhood and see if we could come up with leads for sales. The very first lady we encountered was outside working in her garden, a real talker who had already done up her own preneed after her husband died. She sent us on our way with three different flower starts apiece.

The next house had a husband and wife cleaning out the flower beds. After talking with them, they gave Bernice the names of their aunt and uncle who had yet to do any preplanning. The next-door neighbor called us over for fresh strawberry shortcake. We left with the recipe.

Three doors down, a guy was out in his driveway working on his truck. I introduced myself and Bernice. "I'm Tom Dillon," he said, "and my wife and I have been talking about getting some things started. We have two children with disabilities, so we'll have to plan for four people. What do we need to do first?"

"Cemetery spaces," was my reply, "then vaults, memorials, and funerals."

"How much for four spaces?" Tom asked.

I gave him the figure, and he said, "Write it up." Tom got his checkbook out of the glovebox, and I wrote up the contract on the hood of his truck. Tom handed me the check and thanked us for stopping by.

Bernice and I went back to the car, returning to the office with flower starts, recipes, leads, a contract, and new friends. I told Bernice, "This day was better than winning at the casino."

"Cha-ching," she agreed, laughing.

LOVE IS THE BEST GUIDE OF ALL

After enjoying another lunch out at Jenny's Cafe with Bernice on yet another gorgeous spring day, we both that decided that once again, we did not want to return to the office. Given that our first time out cold calling had proved so fruitful, we decided to give it another go. "Let's go to the outskirts of town this time," Bernice said. Everyone's outside enjoying the weather. Why not us?"

We didn't even have to go that far. Just a couple blocks down from Jenny's, we found two couples outside working on their gardens. I parked at the curb, and we got out to say hello and introduce ourselves. It turned out that these two couples had already made their arrangements at the church cemetery down the road.

We then crossed the street, where an older gentleman was digging up weeds from his flower bed in front of his gorgeous two-story home. I introduced Bernice and myself and informed him we were from the cemetery down the road. He responded with a smile. "My wife, Doris, is buried there. I'm Harry."

We chatted a few more moments before he invited us to come inside. "I want to show you the kitchen cabinets I made for my wife before she passed," he said.

Harry led us into his kitchen, where Bernice and I encountered the most gorgeous kitchen cabinets we had ever seen. "I retired about five years ago and was just so bored," he explained. "Doris took it upon herself to buy me a whole garage full of saws and woodworking equipment. I had no idea how to use any of them. I was a dentist for over forty years.

"Doris said, 'I want a bookcase, a new desk, and then I want new kitchen cabinets. You, Harry, are the smartest man I know. You can figure it out.'"

Bernice and I smiled, anxious to hear the next part of this story.

"I thought she was crazy, but after I made the bookcase and desk, I was really enjoying myself, so I got started on the kitchen cabinets. About halfway through, Doris went for a physical. When they ran tests, they found out she had terminal cancer. She refused any treatments. I finished the cabinets, and she was thrilled with them. She said she loved them and was so proud of me for making them." Harry then had to stop and wipe the tears from his eyes.

I glanced over at Bernice and found her daubing her own eyes with a tissue.

"Doris always called me Hon. She said, 'Hon, I want you to build me a cherry bedroom suite. I want to be surrounded by the beauty of the wood and feel the love we've shared with each other as I pass.'"

It was becoming harder and harder to not crumble right there on the floor. Bernice was trembling, trying to keep her emotions intact.

"I got the chest, bed, and nightstands done, then moved Doris into the bedroom. When she got really sick, I refused to leave her side. I hired a nurse and housekeeper to help me take care of her. My beautiful wife was gone six weeks later. I finished the dresser and cedar chest after her funeral."

Bernice and I had tears running down our cheeks. "Would you ladies like to see my wife's bedroom suite?" Harry asked.

"Sure," Bernice and I said in unison.

Harry had us walk up the stairs in front of him. At the landing, we headed straight into the master bedroom. Never in my life had I seen a more strikingly elegant bedroom suite. We were taken by the beauty of the glistening cherry wood. The heart-shaped headboard emanated the love that was put into its creation. Maybe it was the depth of the love put into it that made this furniture so beautiful. I can honestly say that I have never seen anything that compared to its beauty.

We left thanking Harry for sharing his life and his beautiful wood creations with us. Bernice and I walked slowly back to my car. After a long pause and many tears, I said, "Aren't we the lucky ones? Only cemetery people would get invited into a person's whole house, especially the bedroom, and hear the best love story ever."

IT ALL CAME OUT
IN THE WASH

Halfway through doing my laundry on a Sunday evening, my washing machine broke down. I called the repairman on Monday morning only to find out he wouldn't be available to come out until the following Monday. I was off on Wednesday, so Wednesday morning, I loaded up my family's laundry and headed to the Laundromat. I was wearing my cemetery name tag because I had an appointment down the road from the Laundromat a couple hours later.

There were two women in the Laundromat who appeared to be related. One looked to be in her late seventies with her silver hair piled on top of her head and dressed in a faded old checkered dress. The other one who was doing all the work looked to be in her late fifties. She was dressed in faded blue jeans and a baggy red sweatshirt.

The older lady called out, "I have my space at your cemetery right next to my husband, Charles! He passed about fifteen years ago. God rest his soul."

Automatically, I told her I was sorry for her loss. I then proceeded to ask her if she had all her own final expenses in place. "No," she said shaking her head. "My daughter and I live on a fixed income. We have insurance that'll take care of everything when the time comes."

I advised her to take the time to write everything down before she passed so that her family knew her wishes.

"My name is Ada, and this is my daughter, Esther," she said. "Give me your card and I'll call you. We'll set a time to meet with you the next time we go out to visit Charles's grave."

I handed them each a business card then hurried off to get my laundry done so I could get ready for my appointment.

Five days later, I received a call from Esther. "I found my mother dead this morning in her bed. She was fine when she went to bed last night, but she just didn't wake up this morning. Can you please guide me on what to do? Your funeral home just came by to pick up her body. I'm supposed to meet with them tomorrow, but I feel so lost."

"Do you have other relatives that can come and stay with you?" I asked.

"My neighbor's here, and she said she would stay with me until my brother arrives from Tennessee," Esther replied, sounding confused.

"You and your brother will go to the funeral home in the morning, and I'll meet you at the cemetery office after that. We'll get it all taken care of, Esther. Don't worry," I said.

"Thank you," she sobbed and hung up the phone.

Esther walked in the next day in her faded jeans, cowboy boots, and blue-checked shirt. Beside her was a tall gentleman with deep-brown eyes wearing a black three-piece suit. He extended his hand and introduced himself as Charlie, Esther's brother. Never would I have put them together to be brother and sister. They were complete opposites in looks, mannerisms, dress, and personalities.

After going over all the paperwork with them, I asked how they wanted to settle the charges. Charlie pulled a checkbook out of his vest pocket. After I gave him the receipt, he said, "Esther should have the insurance check in a couple weeks. She's to take care of all her own final expenses with that money, and I would appreciate it if you would see to it that she gets that done."

I told them I would call Esther in two weeks to see how she was doing and to get all her prearrangements set up.

Two weeks later, I called Esther, and she told me to come on out. I drove up to a large two-story farmhouse with a sizeable vegetable patch running the entire length of the driveway. Esther met me at the door and invited me into the kitchen. "Forgive the mess," she said. "I'm trying to go through all these boxes Mom collected. She saved everything for a rainy day. We grew our own vegetables, raised and butchered a hog and cow every year. We had to raise chickens because we needed eggs, and we sold eggs and vegetables every year to get by."

I nodded.

"I thought the only thing in these boxes were canned goods, but so far, I've found three thousand dollars in ten different boxes. I found ten thousand dollars in six old purses and another four thousand dollars in cookbooks packed in boxes."

She walked over to the kitchen faucet to take a drink of water. "I'm so upset I could scream," she said, trying to contain herself with sips of water. "All those years, we had to go to the Laundromat because we supposedly couldn't afford a washer and dryer. We could never take a trip anywhere, even to see Charlie, because we supposedly couldn't afford it. Yet Mom had money stashed everywhere for that rainy day."

"What are you going to do with all this money?" I asked as I finished up her paperwork.

"First, I'm paying you for all my cemetery needs and my own funeral. Second, I'm buying a washer and dryer. I'm never going to the Laundromat again. Third, if I find any more money, I'm taking a cruise. I'll be giving all those fresh vegetables to the food pantry and all the canned ones, too, if they want them. I have to go through everything, which will take me a year because this is a twelve-room house. Then I'll put the house, its contents, and the land up for sale and buy myself a small house in town."

"That sounds like a well-thought-out plan," I said.

"I've spent my entire life taking care of Mom and Dad. Now I'll spend the rest of it taking care of me."

I had her sign the papers and gave her a receipt for the cash she gave me and wished her all the best. Pulling out of the driveway, I prayed, "Lord, please let her go on a cruise and have the time of her life. She deserves it."

TALES OF GRIEF

GRIEF CAN CAUSE DEATH

Katie, an immensely popular sixteen-year-old beauty queen in our community, had gotten into a fight with her boyfriend because he thought they should be dating other people. They had been going together since she was eleven. After school that day, Katie went home and called her mother. "My world is gone," she sobbed hysterically. "I have nothing left to live for."

"It's okay, honey, we'll work through this," her mother, Lois, said, trying to calm her down, but Katie was inconsolable.

Immediately after the phone call, Lois left work to go home to be with her daughter. When Lois arrived home, she found Katie lying in a pool of blood on the living room floor, dead from a self-inflicted gunshot wound to her chest. She used her father's shotgun that he kept right next to his bed.

When Lois and Bill Baker walked into the funeral home the next morning, they were so sedated and in such a state of shock that four people were literally holding them up to keep them from falling. They were clinging to each other, staring off into a sea of darkness.

The funeral director offered his condolences and asked them gently if they had given any thought to what they might want to do for their daughter's funeral. They both stared at him catatonically, offering no response, as if he weren't there.

Through tears and unimaginable grief of his own, the girl's uncle James took charge, helping Lois and Bill make the decisions about Katie's funeral and burial.

About a month had passed after the funeral when I started to notice Lois coming daily to visit her daughter's grave, usually around three in the afternoon. She would sit and talk at Katie's gravestone.

Some days it looked like she had a Bible and was reading to her daughter. This went on for over a year.

One day, while out in the Garden of Love, I noticed Lois getting out of her car, so I approached her to ask how she was doing. "I'm all right," she responded with the weakest voice and the saddest brown eyes I had ever seen. Lois had aged considerably in the past year, so much so that the thin bones of her face protruded, exaggerating her sunken cheeks. My own heart was deeply sad because I knew she was still broken and probably always would be.

I reached out my hands to hers. "God has given me a peace that only he can," she said, "but my husband blames God for allowing this to happen to his baby girl."

I squeezed her hands, and Lois let out a deep sigh. "Every night, he sits…he sits in front of the TV and just stares at it. Sometimes it's not even on. He repeats the same thing over and over: 'My baby's in hell because people that take their own life go straight there. I will never, ever forgive God for doing this to my baby.'" Tears welled in Lois's eyes. "He's so tortured that I can't stand it. He has so much hatred and sadness in his heart that I'm afraid it's going to kill him."

Every cell of my being was crying for God to help this poor lady. I felt powerless to help, but I offered anyway. "Please let me know if there's anything—anything at all—that I can do for you, Lois."

"Thank you for listening to me," she said, "and if you could put my husband on your prayer list so that he finds peace, I would be grateful."

I replied that I would put him on the prayer list at my church as well as several other churches in the area. We said our goodbyes, and I wished her well. I walked back to the office feeling utterly dejected, begging God to please help these people.

Six months later, we got the call that Bill had suffered a massive heart attack at work. He was only forty-six years old. I believe that he finally found the peace that had eluded him in life and that he was happily in heaven with his beloved baby girl.

SHOULD HAVE, COULD HAVE—DIDN'T

Three gentlemen walked through the cemetery office doors, reeling with the look of shock. I could tell instantly that they were brothers. They all had the same deep, piercing blue eyes and coal-black hair with a tinge of gray on the temples. One of them had a mustache, and the other two were clean-shaven. "I'm Daniel, and these are my two brothers Andrew and Benjamin. We're here to take care of the arrangements for our father, Gabriel Long."

I introduced myself and ushered them into the arrangement room. "I'm going to pull your father's file, and I'll be right back," I said.

When I returned several minutes later, I heard Andrew talking to his siblings. "I talked to Dad about a month ago, and he said he was doing fine. He was busy trying to take care of Mom's flowers and told me he wasn't doing a good job of it because he kept forgetting to water them."

"I stopped by Dad's a little over two months ago," Daniel added. "He told me he was going to the senior citizens' center every day to play cards and ride the bike."

Benjamin chimed in. "My daughter Jackie was at Dad's a couple months ago to show off the new car she got for graduation. Jackie said she took him for a spin around the block, and he was cracking jokes as always."

Then for what seemed like at least an hour, they all went silent. Daniel was the first to speak up. "Mom will never forgive us," he said, his eyes cast to the floor. "We all three promised her before she died

SANDY DOYLE

that we would check in on Dad and keep an eye out for him. We all know that was her one and only wish."

Andrew spoke sharply to conceal his regret. "We could have done better. We should have gone to visit him once a week. He only lived fifteen minutes away. If uncle Bill had not stopped by to say goodbye to Dad on his way to Florida and found him in his recliner, would it have been *another* twenty days before anyone found him?"

Andrew's lips started trembling and tears flooded his eyes. "Now we can't even say goodbye with a proper funeral because Dad sat in that damn chair so long before he was found that we have to have a closed casket."

"The bigger question is," Benjamin said as he caught the eyes of each of his two brothers, "will we ever be able to forgive ourselves?"

NOT THE RIGHT ENDING
FOR A CARIBBEAN CRUISE

A gentleman walked into the cemetery office looking ghost pale and dazed. He said, "My name is John Petro, and my wife has passed away. The funeral home told me I needed to come here and purchase burial spaces."

I showed Mr. Petro into the arrangement office and asked him if he already owned any spaces. Shaking his head no while daubing his eyes with a tissue, Mr. Petro dropped his head into his hands. "I don't understand why she left me," he sobbed. "My wife was planning my retirement party, and here I now am, planning where she's to be buried."

He lifted his head and caught my eyes. "Yesterday we booked a Caribbean cruise. Can you believe that? We were going to sit on the deck and bask in the beauty of the sun and the ocean. We were hoping to see some whales and dance the night away."

My first thought was that life can sometimes be so cruel. "I'm so sorry," I said. "That's a hard blow."

He nodded. "We never talked about dying. I have no idea what she would want."

"Do you have any relatives buried here?" I inquired.

"Her grandparents are buried in the Garden of Love," he said. "Their names were Emma and Herschel Smith."

I retrieved the map of the Garden of Love and found two available spaces, three rows up from his wife's grandparents. "These spaces are quite close, and they're right near a flowering dogwood tree," I said.

"Oh, Myrtle would love that," he smiled. "I'll take them." Mr. Petro proceeded to write out a check for everything that was needed for him and his wife at the cemetery.

"I'll call you in a couple weeks to make sure everything is to your satisfaction and that you're doing all right and to see if you have any questions," I told him as we walked to the door.

"No," he said. "I may have to go on this cruise if I can't get my money back or if I just need to get away. Call me in about six weeks and we'll talk."

"Okay, then," I said. "Bon voyage."

Six weeks later, I tried to contact him. There was no answer, so I left a message. Two months went by, and I tried to contact him again. Still no answer, so I left another message.

Close to four months later, Mr. Petro walked into the cemetery office and introduced me to his new wife, Dora. Dora had olive skin, big brown eyes, long black hair. She was dressed in a bright violet skirt that ended at her midthigh and a low-cut blouse with violet and white flowers that showed off her cleavage quite well.

I knew Mr. Petro was in his early sixties, and I guessed Dora to be in her early forties. The whole scene screamed red flag, but I squashed the feeling and kept my thoughts to myself. Mr. Petro had a light in his eyes that he definitely didn't have the day we met four months prior. "I want to trade my space in the Garden of Love to a space in that new garden you have…the Garden of Miracles," he informed me.

Danger! Danger! Red flag! Red alert! Why would you do that! my insides screamed.

"I also want to purchase a space there for Dora," he said, beaming at Dora. "It's such a miracle that we found each other on that cruise, so that's where I want to spend my afterlife with her."

I wrote up the contract, summoning up a level of restraint that I wasn't even aware that I had, doing my best not to say anything negative or derogatory, and biting my tongue while Dora was petting Mr. Petro like a kitten.

I hope the sex is worth it, I was thinking. Then I asked God to forgive me for being so judgmental of a person I didn't even know.

Why was I feeling that this just wasn't right? This was one instance where the customer was not right. Still, I did my job, drew up the contract, closed the sale, and said goodbye.

Three months later—to the day—Mr. Petro walks back into the office, looking like he'd been run over by a big truck. His skin was a pale gray, and he looked like he had lost about thirty pounds. Nearly stumbling over to a chair and trembling, he said, "Dora left me, and she cleared out my bank accounts."

Why doesn't that surprise me? I thought. Still, I felt awful for the guy.

Mr. Petro looked down at the floor. "Is there any way I can sell Dora's space back to the cemetery and move my space back beside my first wife?"

I took in a deep breath of frustration, hoping that he didn't notice. I checked to see if the space was still available next to his first wife, and it was. "We can transfer ownership back to the Garden of Love next to your first wife, but you put that one space in the Garden of Miracles in Dora's name, so you don't own it."

"You're telling me that because I put her name on that space just like I did with the bank accounts that she has a legal right to that property?" Mr. Petro was coming unglued right before my eyes.

"Yes," I replied.

"She's gone back to Mexico. She'll never use it. It'll just lay there empty, and no one will ever use it," he said in disbelief, close to tears.

Finally, after a few minutes of contemplation, Mr. Petro said, "This has been an experience that I would not wish on my worst enemy. I just hope I can get over it."

"Me too," I agreed as he walked out the door.

Two months later, the funeral home got the call that Mr. Petro had died in his sleep. Losing a loved one of forty years, finding new love, then having that new love betray you, losing all the money you worked so hard for your whole life—all within the span of one year—was more than Mr. Petro's heart could take. He wasn't that old, and he had seemed pretty healthy from my point of view—before Dora came along, that is.

PETS GRIEVE TOO

Mrs. Denise St. John came into the cemetery office to sign the papers to open and close the grave space for her mother's burial. Denise was a talker, and she told me all about her mother's life as well as her own. She told me how, when her mother got sick, she moved her into her house, quitting her job to devote all her time to her.

When Denise's mother became ill ten years prior, the best medical treatment money could buy couldn't find out what was making her ill. One day, she seemed fine, and the next day, she couldn't eat. Some days she couldn't even walk. "My Mom was such a sweet, loving lady, and she never once complained," Denise explained. "When it got to the point where she had trouble walking or standing, she sat in her chair most of the time, not really eating or talking. She'd just sit around petting our dog Trixie.

"Would the cemetery care if I brought Trixie out to mom's grave after the service?" Denise asked. "All Trixie wants to do is sit in Mom's chair. She won't eat. It's like she's waiting for Mom to come back."

"Of course, bring her out." I replied. "We have people bringing the deceased's pets out all the time. Clients tell me that it seems to help the pet. They seem to understand where their loved one is."

"Thank you so much!" Denise exclaimed. "We got Trixie just a few days before Mom came to live with us, and they became best buddies overnight."

About six weeks later, Denise came into the office, asking to speak with me. When we got into the inner office, she started crying. I handed her a tissue and asked how I could help her. "After mom's funeral, Trixie wouldn't eat or drink, so I brought her out here to Mom's grave. The poor thing laid down on the grave and cried.

When it was time to go, I picked her up and put her in the car, and she whimpered all the way home.

"After about three days, I took her to the veterinarian, who couldn't find any health reasons why Trixie wasn't eating or drinking. He said that grief was the only answer he could come up with and that he had had two other cases where a pet had grieved itself to death.

"I took Trixie home that day and laid her in Mom's chair. Four days later, Trixie died right there," she said, tears flowing down her cheeks.

Denise brought out a tissue to wipe her face. "I had Trixie cremated, and I want to have her ashes scattered on mom's grave. How much would this cost me?" she asked.

I took a deep breath, knowing my answer wasn't going to land well. "The cost is not the issue," I explained. "In our state and in this cemetery, the law prevents animals from being buried or scattered here. Most states have laws prohibiting animals and humans being buried together. Because of the growing numbers of pets being considered family, a few states are changing the law. I'm sorry to say that it hasn't happened yet in our state."

Denise looked at me like I was crazy. "I have never heard of anything so ridiculous," she huffed. "Trixie grieved herself to death over my mother. They belong together."

"I understand completely," I said with compassion, "but I can't change the law."

"Well," she sniffed, "I can assure you that they will be together if I have to disinter my mother or come out here in the middle of the night to scatter Trixie on top of Mom's grave and stomp the cremains down in the ground. No one but I will ever know." And with that, Denise got up and bolted for the door.

I'll never know if Trixie's cremains were scattered on Denise's mother's grave, but I do know that we are all connected and that Trixie now resides with the lady she loved so much, whom she just couldn't live without.

THE WORST IN PEOPLE

Over all the years I worked at the cemetery, I discovered that death could either bring out the best or the worst in people. Death would bring families closer together, or it would separate them. The feelings of hurt, guilt, and grief make people behave in ways that they normally would not. The Smith family was a perfect example.

Three women walked into the office arguing in loud voices. I introduced myself and asked them how I could help them. A robust tall lady dressed in a green cashmere suit said, "My name is Eunice, and our mother has passed away."

"Our mother was Mildred Smith, and I am Bernice, the oldest daughter." Bernice was dressed in a red wool suit with diamond earrings and a diamond pendant.

"My name is Joyce, the youngest, and I'm the executor of Mom's estate."

"Only because you forced her to sign it when she was sick and didn't know what she was doing," Eunice piped up.

"I did no such thing," said Joyce, her pudgy face growing redder by the minute. "If you had ever bothered to visit her, she might have put your name on the paperwork. But no, you couldn't find one measly hour a week to spend with your own mother."

Bernice said, "Joyce, I will never forgive you for not calling us sooner so we could be with Mom as she passed."

Joyce's face was now a deep scarlet. "I called you as soon as the hospice nurse told me Mom was close to death and that it was time to call you. You both live fifteen minutes away. Why did it take you an hour to get to the house?"

"Unlike you, Joyce, we have lives and responsibilities," Bernice said with a nasty tone.

Joyce's now-crimson face shouted, "I promised Dad I would take care of Mom because he knew you two were too selfish to care what happened to her."

I knew I was going to have to get control over this situation soon before I had to call the police. "Your parents prepaid for everything," I said. "All I need is for Joyce to sign the papers, giving us permission to open and close the grave." I gave them my card and told them I would be in touch to make sure everything was to their satisfaction and to see how they were doing.

About two weeks later, Joyce came into the office. She wanted to write up a contract for all her own final expenses. "I want to be buried next to Mom," she said. "I took care of her the last five years, and I know Dad bought four spaces, so I would love to be buried next to her. I want to get everything taken care of now because the way my sisters are acting, they would probably put me in another cemetery or cremate me and throw me in the dump."

I checked her parents' file to confirm that they were the sole owners of the four burial spaces. They had left no instructions on what was to be done with the two extra spaces.

"Joyce," I began, "because there were three heirs, two of the three must sign affidavits giving up their right to those spaces. I'll be glad to send out a form letter to your sisters for them to sign, relinquishing their rights to that space."

"They both have spaces out here with their husbands," Joyce protested. "They'll never use them."

"I understand," I said, "but your parents owned those spaces. After their death, because they didn't specify what to do with them, the spaces became available to all surviving children, not just you."

After Joyce left, I immediately mailed out the form letters for Bernice and Eunice to sign. A week later, Bernice and Eunice stomped into the office, demanding to speak with me. Eunice said, "Joyce won't let us into our mother's house or have anything that belonged to Mom. Mom always said that Joyce would get the house and that we would get her antique jewelry. There's no way now we'll be signing anything so she can be buried next to Mom!"

Bernice said flatly, "Joyce can be buried in space four, but space three can sit empty. Dad's in space one, Mom's in space two, space three will remain empty, and Joyce can be in space four. That's the way we want it."

Bernice and Eunice signed the papers specifying Joyce's use of space four, and they immediately marched out of the office as if they had won the battle. I took a deep breath and asked for guidance from above then called Joyce to ask her to come out to the cemetery the next day.

When I told her the outcome of the meeting with her sisters the day before, she nodded her head and looked so deeply sad that I thought she'd explode into tears.

Joyce signed all the paperwork and wrote a check for all her final expenses. As she was nearing the door, she turned and said, "I'm sorry you had to see me and my sisters at our worst. Mom and Dad never raised us this way. I tried to explain to my sisters that the lawyer said nothing was to go out of the house until the estate was settled. Mom put my name on the bank accounts and the house. She told me the girls could come into the house and take whatever they wanted, including the antique jewelry she had inherited from both her grandmothers.

"Now, I'll be selling the house, its contents, and the antique jewelry, and will be putting everything into a trust for Habitat for Humanity. I'll give my sisters a real reason to hate me now." Then she turned and rushed out the door.

I slumped into my chair, drained by this whole experience, closed my eyes, took in some deep breaths, and thought, *Everyone lost this battle.*

NO ONE UNDERSTANDS

On a blustery, rainy October day, Mr. and Mrs. Rogers walked into the cemetery office, looking like they were living their worst nightmare, and they were. Both of their sons, ages twenty-five and thirty, had drowned in the local reservoir. One son had fallen off their small boat into the water; the water, being so cold, made it hard for him to breathe. The older son jumped in to help his brother only to have the air knocked out of his lungs as well, thus drowning them both.

Mrs. Rogers picked out two spaces for their sons and two spaces for her and her husband. She took charge of all the other arrangements as well because Mr. Rogers just sat there with a cold glare in his eyes, his jaw set in stone. Every time Mrs. Rogers or I asked him anything, he stared out into the abyss and wouldn't communicate.

Two days later, the funeral home called to say that a fifty-car funeral procession was on its way to the cemetery from a big church across town. I went out to witness the burials. After the committal service, I watched many people approach Mr. Rogers to offer condolences and hugs, but he stopped them in their tracks with a cold glare. Throughout the entire service, he never spoke a word to anyone.

Three weeks later, I made my follow up call with Mrs. Rogers to see how they were doing. She revealed that they were not doing well at all. "My husband refuses to eat," she said. "He quit his job. He starts drinking hard alcohol from the time his feet hit the floor in the morning until he passes out at night."

"I'm so sorry you're experiencing this," I said. "I can give you the names of some people who deal with grief. Two or three are ministers."

"Thank you, but no," she replied. "I can't take a chance on what he would do if someone did come out. Our own minister has been here three times. The last time, my husband told him to get the hell out and to never come back, that if he ever came back onto his property, he would shoot him."

I could tell by her voice she was crying, and I found myself holding back my own tears.

"My husband told me and our minister, 'I have nothing to live for, and I don't want to listen to crap from people who think they understand what I'm going through. No one understands the loss and the guilt I feel. If I had gone with them that day, I could've saved them. But no, I was at your church, helping set up a craft show. Those boys were my life. Where was your God?'"

"Is there anything I can do for you?" I asked.

"Could you please pray for me?" she said, sobbing. "Right now, I just can't find the words."

I told her I would and that I would put them on a prayer chain. I hung up the phone and let my tears come, all the while praying for Mr. and Mrs. Rogers.

Three months later, on a Monday morning about 10:00 a.m., the funeral home called to report Mr. Rogers's passing. On the death certificate was written, "Cause of Death: Alcohol Poisoning." It should have said, "Loss, Grief, Guilt."

VISIT FROM THE DEAD

On the day after Christmas, a lady shuffled into the cemetery office on a walker with her oxygen tank tied to it. She had snow-white hair piled on top of her head and a soft glow to her withered face. She said, "My name is Myrtle Wiggins. The funeral home told me I needed to come here to pay for the opening and closing of my husband, Merlin's, burial space. He passed away yesterday on Christmas day."

Myrtle pulled a tissue from her walker bag to wipe her tearing eyes. "He wasn't even sick. He was the one taking care of me and our children. I have no idea how we'll survive without him."

While filling out her paperwork, I asked Myrtle how many children she had, silently wondering why they weren't here with her right now. "We had two children," she said. "Our son is in the nursing home with special needs. Our daughter is a single mother trying to raise four children." Myrtle daubed her eyes again. "We're all going to miss Merlin. He was such a good man."

Our transaction complete, I walked Myrtle back to her car, and she thanked me over and over for my help. As I watched her drive away, the thought hit me that it wouldn't be long before she would be back here for her own burial.

Two weeks later, I called to check on her. "Oh honey," she sighed. "I don't think I'm doing so good. You'll probably think I'm crazy, but Merlin comes to me every night and wants me to come with him. He says it's so beautiful where he is and that he needs me there with him. Every night, I say, 'No, our children need me,' and every night, he says he needs me more. Every night, we go through the same thing. I can't get any rest. My daughter thinks I've lost my mind."

Myrtle hesitated waiting for an answer. "Have you ever heard of such a thing?" she asked hopefully. "Spirits coming back to visit loved ones?"

"Yes, I have," I responded. "Different people have told me that a loved one has shown up once and sometimes talks to them, but I've never heard of anyone showing up every night."

"Thank you. That makes me feel a little better," Myrtle said. "Every night, I drift off to sleep, and Merlin comes and tickles the bottoms of my feet until I'm fully awake. He stands at my bedside smiling and holding out his hand for me to come with him. He stands there until I tell him to go away so I can get some rest. When he finally leaves, I can't get back to sleep. I'm so exhausted. I haven't had a good night's sleep since he passed."

I suggested she call her doctor to see if they could give her something to help with her sleep. "That's a good idea because I'm so very tired," she murmured. "I think I'll go try and take a nap now. Thank you."

Two days later, the cemetery got the call from the funeral home that Myrtle had passed. I wasn't at all surprised and found myself hoping that Myrtle had found the beauty and peace that Merlin had promised her.

SORRY WON'T
BRING HER BACK

On a May day when spring was just coming out in full bloom, a big burly man charged into the cemetery office. He was well over six feet tall with shoulders nearly as wide. His face was set in stone and seemed to say, "I'll mop the floor with you if you get in my way."

Right behind him walked a gorgeous blond lady with emerald-green eyes and a linen suit that matched her eyes perfectly. "I'm here to take care of things for my mother-in-law, Cora Weatherly," he said, "because of her incompetence to do so. I'm Burt West, and this is my wife, Connie West."

I showed them into the arrangement office and pulled Cora's file. Five years prior, Cora had purchased a single burial space and had paid for nothing since. There weren't even any notes in the file to indicate that she'd been contacted to purchase the rest of her preneed arrangements.

I conveyed to the Wests that Cora still needed a vault, opening and closing of the burial space, and a memorial. "How much is this going to cost me?" Burt blasted.

I told him seven hundred dollars for the vault and vault installation, five hundred dollars for the opening and closing of the grave, and one thousand dollars for a memorial. Burt jumped up and started pacing the room like a lion. "You're making a profit off people on the worst day of their life! You're making a profit off the death of my mother-in-law!" he yelled.

I found myself reaching for the emergency button under my desk because, for the first time in my life working as a cemetery counselor, I felt afraid. Then just like that, Burt sat back down, took out his checkbook, and wrote a check for everything. "You, lady, are a lowlife," he sneered. "You're out here robbing people on the worst day of their lives. I think you're lower than any car salesman I've ever dealt with."

I never said a word. I had no words and felt that if I said anything, it might make things worse for both me and Connie.

Burt tore out the check from its book with a fury and threw it at me. Then he turned to Connie and sneered, "You owe me. Now let's get out of here." And with that, he got up and stomped his way to the door.

Connie looked at me and whispered, "I'm so sorry."

I asked her what she wanted printed on her mom's memorial.

"Just put roses around it with the words, 'Rest in Peace, Momma,'" she said as she rushed out the door to catch up with Burt.

After they left, I felt like I had been beaten, both physically and emotionally. I couldn't imagine what Connie was feeling. What was her daily life like with this man? If he berated her so badly in public, imagine what he did in private. Did he beat her? All I knew was I was glad I'd never have to deal with him again, or so I thought.

Two weeks later, Burt walked back into the office, looking unrecognizable, a shell of the beast I'd encountered two weeks before. He was stooped over, unshaven, and he looked like he'd been in the same clothes for days. "My Connie has committed suicide," he stammered. "I need to purchase two spaces and pay for both of our final expenses here at the cemetery."

I showed Burt into the arrangement office and pulled the map of the Garden of Prayer, where Connie's mother was buried. I pointed out two spaces in the row just above where Cora was buried. "I'll take them. Just write up the contract for everything we need," he said, sobbing.

I finished up the paperwork and gave him the total for all the expenses. This time, there was no blustering. Burt reached into his pocket, pulled out a wad, and paid cash for everything. As he was leaving, he said, "I don't understand why she would do this. She knew I loved her, and I worked all the time to give her anything she might want or need."

"We never truly know what's going on in other people's minds or hearts," was my reply.

Burt found no solace in what I said and simply shook his head and left.

I closed my eyes and thought of Connie's beautiful emerald eyes having the life crushed out of them slowly by Burt's hateful and berating words, and my tears flowed freely down my face and off my chin.

Two days later, I was on duty to lead in the funerals and to witness the burials, including Connie's.

Everyone had left but the minister, funeral director, and Burt. After a few minutes of Burt standing there still as a statue, I told him that we were about to lower the casket into the vault and fill the space with dirt. Burt nodded.

When Connie's grave was over halfway filled with dirt, Burt came out of the trance he was in and threw himself into the grave, sobbing uncontrollably. He kept saying over and over and over, "I'm so sorry, Connie. Please come back to me."

The minister and the funeral director picked Burt up and placed him in the back of the family car, dirt and all.

As the car disappeared around the bend, the grounds crew completed filling the grave and finished by placing the sod on top.

For many evenings after that day, on my way out of the cemetery after work, I saw Burt lying on top of Connie's grave. Maybe he was crying or begging forgiveness or pleading with her to come back or trying to make sense of why she couldn't handle life with him anymore. I'll never know for sure, but I was certain that I'd never have to interact with Burt West ever again.

GETTING BACK AT
THE EX-WIFE

Knowing people for years, witnessing a tragedy in their lives unfold, and then noticing how they handle grief and what unfolds in their lives afterward has always been fascinating to me. My time at the cemetery was teaching me that tragedy and grief either bring people closer or separate loved ones forever. The following is a perfect example of what I mean.

I went to high school with Julie, and although we were friends, we weren't close. Tom and Julie Nelson were both teachers in our community. They met in college, married, had three children. To outsiders looking in, their lives seemed so perfect. Tom had moved into an administrator position in the school system. They were heavily involved in school business, their children's activities, and their church.

One day, their youngest son, Kevin, started having severe headaches that became even worse with each passing day. Medical tests revealed that Kevin had an inoperable brain tumor. Within six months' time, he was gone.

Tom came into the office to purchase three mausoleum crypts and entombing with the idea of placing Kevin in the middle one. Ownership of the crypts was put solely in his name, and he planned to occupy the one next to his son, with the other crypt being occupied by whomever he chose.

About three months after Kevin's death, Julie had a nervous breakdown and tried to commit suicide. After some therapy, she moved back home with her parents, leaving Tom and their other two children behind.

Tom filed for divorce on grounds of abandonment and sought full custody of the two older children. He informed the school board that at this time, because of her breakdown, Julie wasn't ready to resume her teaching position. Julie, being on a leave of absence, subsequently lost her job.

Near the end of that year, I was out witnessing a burial when I noticed Julie sitting on a bench out by the mausoleum. After the burial was complete, I walked over to her to ask how she was doing. "I'm okay," she said. "My heart physically hurts, and all I want is to be with my son." She broke down sobbing. "All I asked for in the divorce was the space next to my baby, and Tom refused. No one understands why I couldn't go back to that house. I saw Kevin everywhere. I saw him running to give me a hug, I saw him cajoling me into making him sugar cookies. I saw him in my sleep. I saw him begging me to make the pain go away."

I sat down beside her and took her hand, praying that God would give her comfort. We sat in silence for a while. Finally, she said. "I'll be all right. The therapist told me it just takes time, but I doubt that this is something you ever get over."

Julie got up and walked to her car. I never saw her at the cemetery again.

Ten years later, an elderly couple walked into the office to ask if the cemetery would be interested in buying back their mausoleum spaces. They told me they had moved to Arizona to live close by their son and that they no longer had any use for the spaces. I called my boss to ask if we wanted to buy these crypts back. "Yes," he said. "We only have one empty space left on that side of the mausoleum. Have the office write them a check."

When the transaction was complete and the elderly couple left, check in hand, I looked at the map to see where exactly these mausoleums crypts were located. To my surprise, they were directly under Tom Nelson's crypts. I immediately called Julie and told her about this new development. I informed her that the one crypt was directly under her son's.

After a lot of hesitation, Julie responded. "Thank you, but no. I've decided to be buried next to my mother in another cemetery."

I was surprised at her level of acceptance around the situation. "My son is not there," she stated. "He's in my heart, and that's all that matters. No one can ever take that from me no matter what."

After a moment, she said, "You might call Tom, though. He's remarried and has another son who has a lot of health issues."

I hung up with Julie and called Tom, asking him to come out to update our files and to share with him the news of the crypts. Tom walked in the next day dressed in a gray business suit, a gray shirt, and a royal blue tie. He seemed to have an air about him that everything had to be his way or the highway.

I showed him into the inner office and gathered up some basic information for our files: wife's name, address, phone numbers. I then pulled out the mausoleum map to remind Tom of the placement of the three spaces he already owned. Then I showed him the four crypts located in the row right beneath. "Do you think your current wife will want to be entombed next to your son instead of you?" I asked.

"I'll purchase them all," he said without hesitation.

"Who's going to use the extra spaces," I asked.

"No one," he replied. "I just want to make sure my ex-wife is not entombed anywhere near me or my boy." He wrote out a check for four mausoleum crypts, knowing full well that three of those crypts would never be used.

Sometimes hatefulness and bitterness cost you, was my thought as Tom strolled out the door.

SHE DID IT MOM'S WAY

A frail-looking lady walked through the cemetery doors with four younger versions of herself following her. "My name is Juanita Hull, and I'm here to take care of the arrangements for my husband, Thomas Hull. These are my children Sammy, Sonny, Sandy, and Sophie. I named them after our parents. May they all rest in peace," she said while making the sign of the cross.

Juanita was a small-boned lady who looked like the slightest wind could easily blow her over. Her puffy white curly hair added height to her tiny frame.

I showed them all into the arrangement office. "Do you have burial spaces here?" I inquired.

"No, they have nothing," Sandy piped up.

"They should have had all this taken care of years ago," Sonny remarked.

"Sonny, shut up," Sophie spouted. "It is what it is."

Sammy chimed in. "The issue is that Dad made the remark once that this cemetery was so beautiful that he wouldn't mind being buried here, but how much is it going to cost Mom?"

I asked Juanita where she would like to be placed in our cemetery. "We have the Gardens of Hymns, Miracles, Masonic, Peace, Love, and Prayer," I offered.

"The Garden of Prayer," she answered quickly. "I've been a prayer warrior all my life. That's where I want to be."

"But, Mom," Sonny said, "Dad was a mason. He should be in the Masonic Garden."

Sandy sternly said, "If Mom wants the Garden of Prayer, that's where they should be."

Sammy asked, "Which garden is the most expensive?"

"It's not all about the money, Sammy," Sophie answered, clearly annoyed.

While the kids were arguing, Juanita leaned in to ask me, "Do all families fight and argue like this at the loss of a loved one? I'm having trouble believing these are my kids."

"Not always," I replied. "Death seems to bring out the best and the worst in families. Death can bring a family closer or split it up. Children feel helpless at death. Sometimes, they take their anger, hurt, and frustration out on the people they care most about."

Juanita nodded in understanding, closed her eyes, and made the sign of the cross. Then she turned her attention back to her children. Suddenly, she was no longer frail. "I know you kids are hurting and you don't know how to handle this situation right now, but I don't need this fighting and arguing right now, and neither do you."

She looked each one of them dead in the eye, her brow furrowed in serious intent. "If I hear any more fighting or bickering, I'll call the police and have you all removed from my home, the funeral home, and the cemetery. This is not about what your father would want. He's gone. It's about what I want and need now that's important. I have insurance and plenty of money to handle everything. Your father and I did not raise you to act this way."

Then in a softer tone that seemed more like the mother she was, Juanita ended with, "If this is not acceptable to you, then please go home. I've been through enough. Do you all understand?"

Sammy, Sonny, Sandy, and Sophie all hung their heads in shame, and not a one of them said another word. Juanita acted like the matriarch that she was, and together, she and I wrapped up all the details. "Give me two weeks and then call me," Juanita said. "I'll finish up everything else on my own. I won't be leaving the smallest detail for them to fight about."

LEFT WITH NOTHING
BUT DEBT

Anger, hurt, and bitterness can all mix together with the grieving process, as it did with Kimberly Copland, a lady of around fifty-four, whose husband, Bill, had died of a sudden heart attack. Mrs. Copland and her two grown sons Ned and Ted came out to the cemetery on a sunny Saturday afternoon to set his arrangements.

Mrs. Copland had strawberry blond hair and a gorgeous golden tan. Because she was in a daze, Ned wrote out the check for all expenses. Ted said, "We'll let Mom pick out the memorial then pay for her space when the insurance check comes in."

Mrs. Copland shook her head in agreement and didn't say a word.

About a month later during our check-in phone call, Mrs. Copland said, "Come on out to the house because I'll never be returning to the cemetery again."

I thought that was a little strange and told her to expect me in an hour. When I arrived at the address, I found an impeccably land-scaped, beautiful, gray two-story brick home in an area close to the college in our town. In the driveway sat a big bass boat and a brand-new silver Cadillac. Mrs. Copland was sitting on the front porch, waiting for me. "What a gorgeous car that is," I said.

"It's for sale," she said bitterly, "the house, the contents, that damn bass boat, and the new car he just had to have before he decided to die. The realtor and auctioneer are coming out next week, so if you're really interested in the car, just let me know.

"My husband was a very selfish man. He wouldn't let me work. He'd never discuss finances with me. He bought this house, this car, this boat. Bill always said, 'Women's place is in the home, raising children.' With Bill, it was all about appearances."

I nodded understanding.

"He left me with a huge pile of debt and a measly fifty-thousand-dollar insurance check. I can't draw his reduced social security until I'm sixty. I get half of his retirement at age sixty-two. He had no right to leave me in this situation. He just couldn't live long enough so I could get his full retirement, could he?" she practically spat.

After a couple minutes of silence, Mrs. Copland's anger started to break, and she became a bit softer. "No, he goes and dies," she said, tears streaming down her cheeks. "I'll never forgive him for the position he's put me in.

"Write up the memorial for him, put a boat on it with the words 'Gone but not Forgotten.' I only want a small single one. At this time, I don't believe I want to be buried next to him. If it weren't for my boys, he wouldn't even get a memorial."

I wrote up the memorial, she wrote me a check, and I wished her well. As I got in my car and headed back to the office, I found myself wondering how many women have no control over their lives, their finances, their decisions, or their bodies. The answer came quickly "More than you'll ever be able to count."

BROKEN LIFE

Even after working at the cemetery for over twelve years, I was still sometimes amazed at the different stories that evolved over time with families. This story is one of them.

Two young men of around thirty walked into the cemetery office holding on to a beautiful blond lady. The older of the two said, "We're here to make arrangements for Mason Bilbray, my father."

I showed them into the arrangement room, introduced myself, and learned that I was dealing with Joan Bilbray and her sons Lucas and Logan. Joan looked at me and said, "I tried to get Mason awake, but he wouldn't wake up. I tried CPR, but he still wouldn't wake up." She shook her head, and her tears started flowing. She kept sobbing the same words over and over. "I shook him. I tried to wake him. I did CPR, but he wouldn't wake up."

I gently took her hand from across the desk and said, "There was nothing you could have done. It was his time to leave."

Joan hung on to my hand for a few minutes as the tears continued to roll down her face. I handed her a tissue and asked if her family had any relatives buried in our cemetery. "Mason's parents are in the Garden of Psalms," she said.

I pulled the map of the Garden of Psalms and found four spaces under a tree about three rows from Mason's parents.

"I'll take them," Joan said quickly. "I only need two, but I feel I need to buy four. Maybe Mason's brother will want the other two."

Joan paid for Mason's space, vault, opening and closing. I told her I'd put everything else on hold and that I'd get back with her in a couple weeks to finish everything else up. She nodded agreement. "Oh, and we signed the papers last night to sell our house," she said. "The people are from out of town, and they want to take possession within thirty days. I may have to move quickly. Can you call me in about six weeks?"

"Yes, I'll make notes to call you then," I replied.

Six weeks later, I called Joan, and she gave me the address of her new condo on the north side of town. While pulling into the development, I realized these were all brand-new, elegantly designed condos. When I entered Joan's, everything was sparkling new and luxurious. I commented on how beautiful everything was. "Yes," she smiled. "I bought everything new. I either sold or gave away thirty-five years' worth of accumulations. The people who bought our house said they couldn't give me any extra time before taking possession of the house.

"In one night, my whole life changed. Mason and I signed all the papers for the sale of our home, went out to eat, and made plans for our future. Mason was going to take an early retirement, and we were going to buy a condo here to be close to our grandchildren and a condo in Florida for the winters."

Joan grabbed a tissue to wipe away her tears. "Because that one night changed everything, I decided to change my *whole* life," she said. "I have nothing to remind me of my previous life, except memories, and no one can take those away from me. I have my sons and grandchildren, and that's all I care about."

Leaving Joan's, I felt that her attitude was good and felt confident that she would create a new and fulfilling life.

Three months later, Joan walked through the cemetery doors with Logan, her oldest son, looking like she had had all her blood drained completely out of her body. She had easily aged twenty years in three months' time. When she saw me, she broke into a million pieces. I helped Logan get her into the arrangement room into the wingback chair.

When she gained a little control, she said, "My youngest son, Lucas, hung himself last night. He left a note, saying that he couldn't live without his dad and that his life had lost its meaning. I don't know what to do. I feel like my heart is crumbling. Can you help me?"

Joan sobbed even harder, and I closed my eyes, asking for guidance to help her and for comfort for her. I said, "You have two extra spaces. Do you want to use one of them?"

"Yes, put him by me," she said through tears. I want everything finalized for him because after the funeral, I'll never step foot in this cemetery again unless I'm in a casket myself."

Because I had no words, I proceeded to fill out the paperwork while listening to her softly weeping. When they were ready to leave, I gave her a lingering hug. "A mother is not supposed to bury her child," she said ever so sadly.

"I know," I replied. "I want you to get some professional help when this is over. You've been through a lot of loss."

"I'll think about it," she said, hugging me tighter.

Two years later, Logan walked into the cemetery office asking for me. I led him into the arrangement room, and we sat down. Fearing the worst, I waited for him to speak. "My mom has passed away," he said sadly. "Even though her doctor said she had a very rare autoimmune disease, I'm certain she died from a broken heart.

"After my brother's death, she slept all the time. She refused to go out. She stopped eating," he said. "She wouldn't even come over and play with my children, whom she adored.

"I tried to get her to go to grief counseling, but she refused. She said, 'I don't want to talk about death or even think about it.' I will always believe she died of a broken heart."

"After working here for over twelve years, I know that dying of a broken heart is a real thing," I told him.

When Logan left, I sat looking at Joan's file, thinking of the hug she gave me the last time I saw her and realizing she was telling me goodbye.

CELEBRATION
OF LIFE

HIS WORK WAS DONE

On a Monday afternoon, we were expecting John Farmer and his sons to come in to make final arrangements for Ethel Farmer, his wife, who had passed away the day before. Mr. Farmer walked through the door first. He extended his hand and, with a big bright smile, announced proudly, "These are my sons Brad and Josh. We've come to make sure my beloved wife and my boys' mother is laid to rest as nice as possible. My Ethel suffered so much from cancer these last two years, and we want to plan something beautiful. She was the most beautiful person I've ever seen. We want the very best of everything for her."

I wrote down Ethel's biographical information then showed them into the casket display room. They decided on a white casket with pink roses stitched into the casket panel. John walked over to the display of gowns and pointed. "I want this soft-pink gown with those little rose buttons for Ethel to be dressed in. That's just so her."

I commented on the beautiful choices that they had made. John nodded his head. "My wife was a very artsy person," he explained. "She loved art, color, music. If we could display a couple of her paintings at the calling hours, I would appreciate it. And Ethel would love to have Elvis singing gospel. She loved listening to that man sing."

I was taking notes while he spoke.

"I want to make sure her nails are done in a dark pink," John continued. He handed me a photograph. "This is a picture of Ethel with her hair done the way she liked it. Wasn't she so beautiful?" he said, sighing like a teenager in love.

"She truly was," I smiled, thinking to myself how blessed Ethel was to have had this kind of love.

John pulled out his checklist from his coat pocket. "Oh, and I want a light soft-pink blanket placed over her feet and legs. I don't want her feet getting cold. And the casket spray should be pink roses with five white roses, one for each of my boys and my three grandsons."

"How about a red one for you?" I asked.

"No," he replied sternly, "I don't need one."

Seems a little odd, I thought.

Mr. Farmer checked his list again and handed me a slip of paper. "This is the contact information for the minister, organist, and the soloist." He pulled out another. "And these are the songs I want sung at the funeral. They were Ethel's favorites."

"Is Wednesday all right for the funeral?" I asked.

"No," he replied quickly, "let's do it Friday. That was Ethel's favorite day of the whole week. We always went out to eat every Friday."

He ran through his notes one final time to make sure he had covered all the bases for his wife's funeral. Satisfied that everything for Ethel was complete, he said, "While I'm here, you might as well write up my preneed arrangements too so I only have to write one check."

I looked at him in shock. I had never heard of anyone planning their own funeral while simultaneously arranging their loved one's.

"The difference is," he said, "I want a dark-blue casket with praying hands stitched into the lid. Red roses for the casket spray. The boys will bring you my navy blue suit and red tie. You don't have to have my hair and nails done," he said, laughing. "Same music, minister, organist, same songs."

I gave him a price for both services and he wrote out a check in full. "I have just enough money left over to take my family out to eat tonight," he laughed. "And then my work is done."

He shook my hand and thanked me. "I should have done this a long time ago." He put one arm around each of his sons, and they all walked out the door.

The next morning, the funeral home got the call to go pick up John Farmer's body. After taking his family out to eat that night, John went home and shot himself.

After hearing this shocking news, I replayed everything over in my mind from the day before, looking for signs that I might have seen. But then, John had plans right down to the last detail. I doubt that anyone could have stopped him. John couldn't live without his Ethel. His work was done.

EXIT INTERVIEW

While talking on the phone with a client one afternoon, I noticed a rail-thin lady slowly walking into the office. It looked like every step was taking all her energy. I cut my call short and got up to introduce myself. "How can I help you?" I smiled.

With labored breathing, she whispered, "My name is Marsha, and I'm dying." Tears filled her eyes. "I need to make my final arrangements, so my boys won't have to."

I took Marsha's arm, and together, we walked ever so slowly into the arrangement room. I could feel her bones protruding through her long-sleeve blouse. My heart was hurting for her, knowing from experience that any form of movement was taking every bit of energy she had. The sacrifice she was making to try and protect her boys from more hurt than they were already feeling demonstrated pure love.

I sat Marsha down in a cushioned chair and went to grab a pillow to place behind her back. "All right," I said, handing her a catalog, "let's pick out the casket first."

After some time, Marsha settled on a burgundy casket with white velvet lining. Burgundy and pink roses would be stitched into the lid. "Burgundy is my favorite color," she said with a weak smile. "I have a sweater that same color, and I always wore it with a scarf that had a little pink and burgundy in it. It made the outfit pop."

"That sounds lovely," I said. "Let's use that outfit."

"And I want to be wearing my nurse's pin," she added. "I worked so hard for that." Marsha drew a deep sigh. "It doesn't matter, I guess. I want the casket closed."

"Why is that?" I asked.

148

I don't want my family and friends seeing me bald, and there's no amount of makeup that can hide this saggy skin," she said with great sadness. She held out her hands for me to see. "Look at these flimsy fingernails. I always had my nails done up beautifully."

I placed my hands on hers, and tears started flowing down her cheeks. "I've fought cancer three times and thought I had it beat," she sobbed. "The doctor finally told me to go home and enjoy what life I had left. How do you enjoy life when you're so tired that you can't even get out of bed?"

I smiled softly. "We have a funeral director whose specialty is makeup. I've seen him work miracles to faces that have been bruised, broken, and cut into pieces. He won't have any problem making you look just like normal for your boys."

Her spirits lifted a little. "What about my hair and nails?"

"Do you have a favorite wig, one that looks like your real hair?" I asked.

"Yes, but I've worn it so much, it's beginning to look shabby," she said.

"Not a problem," I countered. "We'll have our hairdresser wash and style it so it looks just like your own hair. We'll also have your nails done, maybe a burgundy to match your outfit, and then put-on white tips."

She smiled. "Can you really do all of this?"

"Yes, we can," I smiled. "It's important to us that your family remember the real you, not the sick you."

Marsha let out a deep sigh and her shoulders finally relaxed. "You don't know how relieved I feel right now."

"Is there any certain music you'd like us to play?" I asked.

"I love classical music, and I want the 'Prayer of St. Francis' played at the end of the service," she said.

"What kind of flowers for the casket spray would appeal to you?" I asked.

"White roses with greenery," Marsha replied, a slight smile in her voice.

"Would you like to have two burgundy roses put in the casket spray for each son?" I asked.

"Yes, please," she responded weakly.

I took down Marsha's insurance information, and we finished up by walking together to her car. She gave me a hug and murmured a thank you.

Two weeks later, the funeral home received the call that Marsha had passed. I felt peace and fulfillment knowing that her sons would get to remember the mother they had known their whole lives before cancer reared its ugly head.

GOING, GOING, GONE

Ed Shoemaker—a well-known businessman, farmer, and auctioneer—passed away one evening after holding a big auction in our community. Well-liked by everyone, Ed never met a stranger. His attitude was, "If I can be successful with only a sixth-grade education, anyone can."

Ed's son Douglas came in to make the final arrangements and was shocked that his father hadn't made any prearrangements. "I just don't understand," he kept saying over and over. "Dad always took care of every little detail. This is so unlike him."

The funeral director offered an explanation. "Every time I said, 'Ed, you need to take care of your final arrangements,' his response was, 'I'm not going to be there. Just let my son do whatever he wants, or throw me in the river. I don't care. Why should I pay for something when I can't enjoy it?'"

Douglas kept shaking his head, confounded by the task before him. "I have no idea what Dad would want. He refused to talk about dying."

"Why don't we get started with some questions," I began. "Did your dad like wood or metal?"

"Wood," was his reply. "Walnut was his favorite. Once he made a rocking chair out of a walnut tree that fell on the front yard."

"Do you know what Dad's favorite color was?" I questioned.

"I don't know," Douglas said. "I never heard him say. Probably blue. He was always wearing a blue suit or blue coveralls with a blue shirt. I don't know if that was his favorite color, but that's all he ever wore."

"Any hobbies?" I continued.

"No hobbies. Auctioneering and farming were his loves, and he didn't do much else." He gave the question a little more thought. "Dad just bought a new green tractor last week with a green riding lawn mower to match," he offered.

"Any favorite flowers?" I questioned.

"Yellow roses and wildflowers," Douglas replied instantaneously. "Dad grew yellow climbing roses all around the yard, and he would take wildflower seeds out into the woods and scatter them."

"What about music?" I persisted.

"Country and gospel, maybe 'Amazing Grace.' I used to hear him and Mom sing that song," he said.

From one moment to the next, Douglas became irritated. "Why all the questions?" he resisted. "I thought we were planning a funeral. I don't understand what his favorite color, his hobbies, or music has anything to do with planning a funeral."

"We just planned it," replied the funeral director with a satisfied smile. "Give us a couple days to get everything organized."

Douglas stood up to walk out the door. "I hope you know what you're doing."

Three days later, Douglas showed up an hour before the scheduled services to find his father laid out in a walnut casket, wearing a blue suit, holding an auctioneer's gavel. The casket's lid had an auctioneer's gavel and base stitched inside. The word "SOLD" was stitched in bold blue letters between the base and the gavel. Yellow roses with blue wildflowers draped the bottom half of the casket, and little green tractors were tied into the casket spray.

The funeral started with "Amazing Grace." At the end, as the casket was being closed and the attendees were exiting, "The Auctioneer" song was played over and over.

The next day, Douglas brought in a check to pay for everything. His face was beaming. "I want to thank you folks for all you did," he began. "I couldn't even envision any funeral representing my father's life. Everything you did captured my father to a T. The casket, the flowers, the gavel. When 'The Auctioneer' song started playing, I had tears in my eyes because dad always talked about how his mother had wanted him to go to school, but he would sneak off and go to the auction barn instead. That's where he learned how to talk fast and get bids out of people. He went to work, saved his money, and went to auctioneering school. Dad always said he thought 'The Auctioneer' song was written just for him."

The funeral director and I looked at each other, happy that we had made such a difference in this man's send-off of his beloved father. Douglas extended his hand to take mine. Smiling broadly, he said, "I don't know how you knew what to do, but thank you. From the bottom of my heart, thank you."

I smiled and said, "It's all in the questions, Douglas. It's all in the questions."

ALL KINDS OF ANGELS

The accidental death of an avid motorcycle rider named Brody had rattled a lot of the folks in our community. According to Brody's obituary, he had survived a brain tumor at age sixteen. A car accident had taken his mother's life five years before.

Although the family chose to use a different funeral home, they elected to have Brody buried at our cemetery. Part of my job at that time was to accompany the casket from the time it entered the cemetery to the time it was put into the vault and the vault was sealed. This day, I would be leading the funeral procession to our chapel as well.

I had been waiting close to an hour when the office radioed me to report that the funeral home had called to inform us that Brody's funeral procession was on its way and that it was an exceptionally large procession at that. Stationed at the cemetery gates, I watched in disbelief as ten motorcycle policemen led the procession. The hearse and family car followed them. Behind them, another thirty cars streamed by. Finally, after all the cars had passed through the gates, a swarm of around twenty-five motorcycles of every color, size, make, and model ensued.

Because I had never seen so many motorcycles in one place in my life, my thought was that we were we being invaded by a motorcycle gang. Once everyone was parked and situated, ten of the motorcyclists retrieved Brody's casket from the hearse and carried it into the chapel, while the others escorted the family into the chapel.

I watched in amazement as every biker removed their helmets and bandannas before the preacher started talking, all of them placing their hands over their hearts. The minister closed with a prayer before turning the service over to the ten pall bearers.

Each pallbearer told a different story of how Brody had impacted their lives. One told of how Brody had started rallies and fundraisers to help families who had a child with cancer. Another spoke of Brody's hosting a yearly hog roast at the fairgrounds to bring them all together. Brody seemed to always be around to help whenever anyone needed anything. I found myself welling up with tears listening to the story of Brody's helping a cyclist who had been mangled in a wreck and how he never left his side until the man was out of danger.

The funeral director dismissed the crowd, except for the ten pallbearers who accompanied me to the burial space. There they stood silently, solemnly, bandannas over their hearts, as Brody's casket was lowered into the vault.

As they slowly exited, each one offered words of thanks to both me and the grounds crew. Then they fired up their bikes and raced out of the cemetery. That day, I realized that angels show up on earth in countless different places and ways. That day, they happened to be riding motorcycles.

CHINTZY OR FRUGAL

A Mr. Coy Davidson had passed away, leaving behind ten children, thirty-two grandchildren, and an unknown number of great-grand-children. Mr. Davidson and his wife had moved to our area about thirty years prior from Tennessee to work in the local canning factory. Mrs. Davidson had died about ten years prior. Mr. Davidson took her back home to Tennessee to be buried in an old family cemetery.

Six of the ten Davidson children, along with their spouses and several grandchildren, had flocked into the funeral home this day to decide on what arrangements would be best for Mr. Davidson. After about thirty minutes of listening to everyone argue as to what their father wanted, what was really needed, and who was going to pay for the funeral, the funeral director had ordered everyone out, except the six siblings.

Arguments persisted, as their father had told one child one thing and another child something else entirely. The only thing everyone agreed on was that he was going back to Tennessee to be buried next to their mother. I looked over at the funeral director and noticed that his face was getting redder by the minute. Finally, he said, "Who's going to be responsible for the bill because that's the person I want to deal with."

No one volunteered. There was a long stretch of silence until finally, the oldest son, Rory, spoke up. "I'll take care of the bill, and everyone else can pay me their share. It's the only fair thing to do."

A few of the siblings nodded in agreement, while the others stared down at the floor.

"I think we should go with a metal casket because that's what Mom had," Glory said sternly.

Morey, who had been sitting there the whole time, not saying a single word, finally piped up. "At the cemetery in Tennessee where Mom is buried, they don't require a vault, so it's crazy for us to buy one when we don't need it."

By this time, I thought the funeral director might be well on his way to a heart attack. His face was beet red, and the veins in his neck were throbbing. Barely able to conceal his aggravation, he said, "You should all know that the vault helps protect the remains as well as the cemetery. It helps keep the ground from settling and caving in. Vaults are made of concrete, metal, and plastic. A vault is very important as it helps to protect the remains from the elements of the earth and weather."

Lori, the youngest of all the children, declared. "Dad always said, 'Dust you are, and to dust you shall return.' We don't need a vault. Just let him return to the earth."

Dorey, looking stone-faced, said. "We don't need a funeral here, either. We can just take him to Tennessee and have everything at the church there. There's no need to have two services."

Everyone shook their head in agreement.

Then Torey spoke up, "What about the friends and family here being able to say goodbye?"

Lori spoke back up. "No one cared enough to go see Dad when he was alive. Why would they want to see him dead?"

Rory looked at the funeral director. "Are you going to charge us to take our dad's body back to Tennessee?"

"Yes," he responded a bit harshly. "Hotel expenses, my hourly rate when I'm at the service, and forty-three cents a mile."

Morey chimed in again, "I won't pay for that."

Rory looked at the funeral director with a glint of defiance in her eyes. "We'll just put the casket in my old truck and take him directly to the church in Tennessee."

The funeral director relented. "All right, but you must sign a release form and pay me for the services I've already performed before I'll release the body to you."

"We'll be here at nine tomorrow morning with your money," Lori said.

And with that, Rory, Morey, and Torey stomped out of the funeral home, followed by Glory, Lori, and Dorey, all of whom shot me and the funeral director cold stares on their way out. The funeral director, by now looking thoroughly wrung out, was shaking his head. "I'm going home to get a beer."

I wondered how Mrs. Davidson ever got her children's names straight. My head was spinning with confusion and exasperation about the six Davidson children that I did meet. I felt relieved that I didn't have to interact with Corey, Carrie, Lorry, and Flory on top of the other six.

At nine sharp the next morning, twenty cars pulled up behind an battered-looking old truck. The Davidson brothers loaded their father's casket into the truck and tied it down. Off they all went to Tennessee, and all I could think of was how on earth was that battered old truck going to make it up and down those winding country roads running through the Smoky Mountains. Would the casket end up in a valley somewhere never to be found, or would it be mashed on the interstate by some shocked motorist seeing a casket traveling down the road?

I said to myself out loud, "What would I do if I ever saw a casket coming down the interstate in a beat-up old truck?"

No answer came. Hopefully I'll never find out. Hopefully, no one else sharing the interstate with the Davidsons that day had to find out either.

THE FROGMAN

On a slow and boring day at the cemetery office, I was thinking about going to the lounge and taking a nap. I knew from experience that when our large cemetery goes quiet for over three days with no activity whatsoever, things are fixing to change and usually in strange ways.

I put my head down on the desk, shut my eyes, and was drifting nicely off into slumber when the intercom buzzed. "There's a gentleman on the phone," reported our secretary, "and he says he needs answers, and he needs them now."

I picked up the phone, introduced myself, and asked to whom I was speaking. "My name is Henry," he said, "and I really need to talk with you. Is there any way you can come out to my house this afternoon?"

I explained to him that I had to be in the office until after five that day but that I could be at his house the next morning at ten.

Pulling into the driveway at Henry's home the next day, I noticed the lush rose garden with different-shaped metal and glass frogs placed throughout the garden. Henry was waiting for me at the front door. He appeared quite thin, and I guessed him to be only in his late forties. I introduced myself and commented on how beautiful his rose garden was. "Yes, I spend a lot of time in my rose garden," he said, smiling.

He showed me into his office, where many curio cabinets stood filled with a variety of sizes, shapes, and colors of glass frogs. Everywhere my eyes landed, I was in awe. Luminous, bright red, orange, brown, blue, green frogs stared back at me. Some of the frogs looked transparent, while others looked translucent. These frogs looked real, and each one was absolutely gorgeous. "This is the reason I called you," Henry explained. "I want to make sure my frog collection is on display at my funeral."

I nodded.

"I created these frogs," he said proudly. "I'm a former glass blower and have put my heart and soul into each and every one of them. I've studied frogs my whole life. Sometimes I wonder if I wasn't a frog in another life because of the passion I have for creating them."

I looked around the room, intrigued. It was like I was onstage with a sold-out audience of frogs. "How many frogs do you have here?"

"There are close to two thousand, and I'd like for part of them to go to an art or glass museum. The other part I want sold. All the proceeds will go to the wildlife preserve in my name. It's so crucial that we protect our wildlife," he said passionately.

"Yes, it is," I agreed.

"And I don't want people wasting their money on flowers, either," he emphasized. "I don't need them. Have them send their money to the wildlife preserve in my memory."

"Do you have children or a lawyer to handle all this for you?" I asked.

"My son lives across the world, and my lawyer is my best friend," he said. "I don't want anyone trying to talk me out of anything. The doctor said I only have a few months to live. I've already used up one month trying to come to grips with it all."

His revelation shocked me, even though I didn't think he was a well man when I first laid eyes on him. Seeing the anguish on his face, my heart broke for him. "I'm so sorry," I said.

"Let's write down exactly what you want, and then I'll make a copy for you to take to the lawyer, a copy to give to whoever is over your estate, and the funeral home will have a copy too," I suggested.

Henry closed his eyes and took in a deep breath, then he let out a big sigh of relief. "Yes," he said, "let's get it done. Thank you."

Trying to contain my emotions, I said, "Between the lawyer, the funeral home, and the executor of your estate, we can make sure your final wishes will be carried out. In the meantime, you can call some glass museums and have their curator come out and get what suits their collections."

I took the paperwork out of my briefcase. "Would you prefer ground burial or cremation?"

Henry entered into deep thought for a few moments before replying. "I want a traditional funeral service and then cremation afterwards. I want my cremains scattered at a wildlife preserve."

I started writing everything down. "How does a wooden casket with a frog stitched into the lid panel sound?" I asked.

"That's okay, since there are to be no flowers," he said.

"We know that some of your frogs will be on display. Would you like to have music played at the funeral and what kind?" I inquired, pegging him for a classical type of guy.

But Henry's musical tastes ran in the opposite direction. "I meditate every morning with recordings of wind and rain softly blowing," he said. "Frogs croaking, ribbiting, clucking, and grunting are my favorite sounds. That's who I am, and I think it says everything about me." For the first time since we met, Henry was smiling.

I found myself amazed at learning about the wide variety of frog sounds. "How do you know that frogs make all these different sounds, Henry?" I asked, just as curious as a little girl. "All I ever heard was a ribbit sound."

Henry was in his element now and was thrilled to explain. "Frog sounds depend on the intent of the frog," he explained. "A frog might be attracting a mate or scaring off a predator. Most of the time, frogs scream when trying to protect themselves."

When I finished up the paperwork, Henry said, "I'm so relieved to get this done. I'll call the local glass museum and my lawyer tomorrow."

I walked out of Henry's house feeling hundreds of frog eyes upon me and wondered, "When Henry passed, would all his frogs be ribbiting or screaming at the loss of their dear friend?"

GET HER OUT OF HERE

The sudden heart attack and death of a prominent midfifties businessman in our area brought out the whole community to pay their respects. Mr. Hall was known by all because he both loved and employed a lot of people. Mr. Hall left behind two sons and a daughter, all in their early thirties; an ex-wife; and a twenty-five-year-old new wife.

My job that day was to greet people as they came into the funeral home and show them to the visitation room. There, Mr. Hall was laid out in a bronze casket, surrounded by flower arrangements which filled the whole room. Mr. Hall's ex-wife and children were standing at the foot of the casket greeting visitors, while the new wife stood at the head of the casket.

The receiving line was long, so I went to check that all was well. Although I saw no problem in that moment, I could feel a storm brewing. Tensions were exceedingly high during the first two hours of visitation because some of the people passing through the line were offering condolences to both the first and second wives, while others snubbed the new wife completely.

I went into the office. The funeral director was going over the plans for the funeral the next day. I relayed to him the scene that I had just witnessed in the visitation room.

While we were talking, the new wife marched in and yelled, "I am paying this bill, and I want my husband's ex-wife out of here! I had to share him with her this last year, but I will not share him with her or her children now. If you must call the police, do it. I want her gone."

She proceeded to hand the funeral director three pictures of her naked. "Make sure you put these pictures in his suit coat pocket just above his heart before the casket lid is closed," she demanded. "I want him thinking of me and all the fun we had, not his ex-wife." She stomped out, saying, "Get her out of here now, or I will."

I glanced at the funeral director, whose face was fire engine red. "The biggest, most expensive funeral in our history, and we have a scene because of a spoiled witch that can only think about herself. I can assure you her husband is dead and doesn't care one bit about her naked pictures, and neither do I."

He got up out of his chair and tossed the photos into the trash can with great force. "Watch the office while I find Mr. Hall's first family and explain to them what's going on," he instructed. "I'll tell them to come back in about two hours to say their goodbyes and not to come tomorrow because you know and I know the witch will have the sheriff here tomorrow."

As it turned out, the sheriff was at the funeral home at nine the next morning but Mr. Hall's first family never showed.

AN OLD COWBOY
GOES HOME

Mayor Tom was a highly respected and much-beloved man who oversaw our tiny community of Fletcher, population: 2,300. During his time in office, he had made it his business to know each and every townsperson by name.

He loved the history of Fletcher, right along with the townspeople, whom he served. Every Memorial Day weekend, he dressed up in full authentic cowboy attire: shirt, pants, belt, pistols, hat, lasso, boots, and spurs.

Along with ten old-timers from the area, Mayor Tom got together to reenact the historical bank robbery that had occurred over one hundred years prior. A video of the reenactment played on a loop in the town hall. Year after year, this event was enjoyed by all and, over time, even turned out to be a tourist attraction.

When Mayor Tom passed away, his wife wanted him buried in his black Sunday suit, holding his Holy Bible. His children and grandchildren, however, wanted him buried in his cowboy attire. In an effort to please everyone, we dressed Mayor Tom in his black suit with his white cowboy shirt and bolo tie. We put his Bible in one hand and his cowboy hat in the other.

Mayor Tom was laid out in a maple-wood casket. The panel in the casket lid depicted a cowboy on his knees, praying. Embroidered on the panel were the words "Going Home." Throughout the calling hours, videos of the bank robbery reenactment from years past played on a loop, delighting the hundreds of townsfolk who came by to pay their final respects.

After the close of the funeral service, Mayor Tom was placed in an antique hearse pulled by four solid-black horses. Behind the hearse, the family, the minister, the pallbearers, and countless townsfolk—all dressed in cowboy attire—walked the mile to the cemetery. Together, they witnessed the lowering of Mayor Tom's casket while singing "Amazing Grace."

I stood at a distance and marveled at the scene before me, thinking what a beautiful tribute this was to a beloved man who brought joy to so many and how his townspeople were forever touched by the inspired life Mayor Tom had lived.

TRIPPIN'

No amount of preparing for a funeral can predict what will happen when emotions are running wild. In the event when poor planning gets thrown into the mix, all bets are off.

A young man named Jarred Barnes, in his midtwenties, had passed away from causes unknown, even though drugs and alcohol had been strongly suspected. Mr. and Mrs. Barnes entered the funeral home in a state of shock to make plans for their son's services. Mrs. Barnes picked out a steel gray casket with a picture of drums embroidered into the lid. Mr. Barnes stared off into space. Every time Mrs. Barnes asked his opinion about details, his reply was, "Whatever."

I stepped in to purposely ask Mr. Barnes, "What kind of music would you like played during the calling hours and the funeral?"

After a few minutes, he returned to the room, blinked, then uttered, "Play that heavy metal music. That's what Jarred loved."

As they got up to leave, I moved toward Mr. Barnes to offer my hand in condolences and was greeted with a hefty whiff of alcohol. Turning to do the same with Mrs. Barnes, I got blasted again.

I told them I could have one of our ministers say a few words at the service if they wanted, or they could call their own minister. Mrs. Barnes said that she would contact a minister who knew Jarred when he was a young boy.

Visitation for Jarred was scheduled for two hours prior to the service. About an hour before, I started to notice many young people coming in. A few minutes later, they were out by their cars, smoking. This scene played out over and over.

The funeral director asked me if I knew the minister's name and what time he was supposed to be at the funeral home. "I'm not sure," I said. "Let me go check."

I went into the visitation room, where I found Mr. and Mr. Barnes standing by the casket and asked them about the minister. Mr. Barnes slurred, "The one we wanted is out of town, so they're sending their youth pastor."

This time, I was nearly thrown back by the overwhelming stench of alcohol coming off him. I held my breath, nodded, and walked away.

Once away from Mr. Barnes, I took in a deep breath, only to find that the unmistakable stench of a skunk filled the room. Alarmed, I marched into the office to tell the funeral director that there was a skunk in the visitation room and that we needed to evacuate the visitors immediately. "Are you really that naive?" he looked at me, astonished.

"What do you mean?" I asked.

"I can guarantee you that ninety percent of the people in there are either drunk, stoned, or both," he said authoritatively. "Either way, they're all on a trip. We'll be lucky to get through this funeral without something strange happening."

The funeral started with the funeral director thanking everyone for coming and helping Mr. and Mrs. Barnes celebrate the life of their son Jarred. "Say Hello 2 Heaven" by Temple of the Dog started playing at the very moment a young green minister walked into the visitation room.

He walked straight to the front of the room, without saying a word to the family. He must've been about as naive as I was. "Heaven is gaining a great young man today," he said with enthusiasm. "Jarred was a loving and giving person who helped many people over the course of his short life. I'm certain that right now, he's walking the streets of gold with Jesus."

Like a shotgun blast, Jared's brother-in-law Sam stood up and exploded. "You don't know what you're talking about! Jarred was the most hateful and selfish drug-dealing degenerate that ever walked this earth!"

The entire bleary-eyed crowd suddenly pulled focus and put all their attention on Sam, whose face was beet red.

"Jarred got half these people here today hooked on drugs, including his own sister!" he spat.

Needless to say, the young green minister was frozen. Sam locked his eyes onto his. "Jarred wouldn't have given Jesus the time of day, let alone be walking the streets with him because he only cared about himself!"

With great indignance, Mr. Barnes jumped up, faltered, and with his best slurred speech, called his son-in-law an ungrateful SOB before lunging and taking him down to the funeral parlor floor. The young green minister, looking like he was about to be sick, foolishly stepped in to separate them and instead ended up having a couple punches thrown in his direction.

By now, about forty people were circling around the two men rolling around the floor, shouting like they were at a professional boxing match. "Go! Go! Hit him again!" yelled one wearing a Metallica T-shirt.

"Punch that fleabag minister!" screamed another with such force that his clip-on tie dropped to the floor.

Two bleached blond twin sisters grabbed each other and shrieked, "Fight! Fight!" in unison.

Soon enough, the entire crowd had joined in the name calling at full voice before the funeral director and the security guard got things calmed down and directed everyone outside, with the exception of a few hangers-on who required special prodding to get them out of the funeral home.

Mr. and Mrs. Barnes sat there in silence, Mrs. Barnes's shame and embarrassment obvious. I took them over some tissues to help with their flowing tears and Mr. Barnes's bloody nose.

Grief, adrenaline, and high emotions ruled that day. I only hope that the young green minister learned his lesson: talk to the family before the service, learn something about the deceased before ever doing a funeral service again.

SHE DID HIM PROUD

A middle-aged father and former captain in the air force who became an airline pilot after his military career ended had been diagnosed with terminal cancer. He refused to accept the doctor's opinion, which gave him less than six months to live. Instead, he sought out at least three other specialists across the country, all of whom gave him the same grim diagnosis.

Captain Craig went on to live another three years, working as a commercial airline pilot right up until two weeks before his death. Cathy, his wife, was a realist who had wanted Craig to preplan for his passing, but Craig was adamant. "No," he told her. "I'm beating this thing."

Captain Craig started working out every day and running five miles, three times a week. He implemented a regimen of herbs, vitamins, juicing vegetables, and fruits every day. Never giving up, he flew all over the world, searching for a cure at every known holy place, from Jerusalem to the Sistine Chapel in Italy.

When people asked how he was doing, his response was always, "Doing good. I'm beating this thing."

One evening, Craig returned home wrung out from a particularly stressful flight in which one of his passengers had died. He went to sleep that night, slipped into a coma, and passed away.

Because we'd been neighbors for some years, Cathy called me to help with some ideas and inspiration for her husband's funeral. "People will be coming in from all over the country," she said. "I want something that our children will remember. Craig was a proud man. I want to do him proud."

Cathy chose a eighteen-gauge soft-blue casket. The interior would be a cream velvet with the air force emblem stitched into

169

the lid panel. She dressed her husband in his blue airline suit. An American flag was draped over the casket. A six-hour visitation was set, and a Catholic Mass would take place the next day, ending with the song "On Eagle's Wings."

After the funeral Mass, about one hundred cars pulled into the cemetery for the grave site service. With friends and family gathered round, the priest blessed the grave with holy water. Everyone stood at attention as seven air force veterans performed the 21-gun salute followed by "Taps" on the trumpet. The flag was folded and handed to Cathy.

As the ceremony was closing, a combat formation with two pairs of aircraft appeared, low enough for all to see. Suddenly, one of the aircraft pulled out of the formation, representing the man missing, while the rest of the formation completed, until they were all out of sight.

The priest ended with a final prayer, and while everyone walked back to their cars, Elvis's version of "My Way" played throughout the cemetery to accompany them.

Captain Craig made his country proud with his service. His wife, Cathy, made him proud with her love.

IN THE NAME OF LOVE

The most rewarding and frustrating arrangement I was ever involved with featured a frail ashen-faced gentleman named Harlan Morris. When Mr. Morris walked through the office doors, I saw a man riddled with pain. I offered my name and was shocked to hear a robotic voice respond with his. Every word created an equal flat sound lacking emotion or intonation. His voice was so weak and difficult to understand that, regrettably, I had to ask Mr. Morris to repeat himself two more times.

He told me that he needed to make sure all his final needs were taken care of. "My trachea was removed because of cancer about three years ago," he explained. "I have an artificial larynx, which turns my vocal cords into sounds. Sometimes the words don't come out right."

I informed him it wasn't a problem, that we could just write down what he wanted. Tears welled in his eyes when he told me he couldn't read or write. "I never went to school. I've worked since I was eight, and I never took the time to learn," are the words that I pieced together between his robotic sobs.

Everything he said was excruciatingly difficult to understand. I had to ask him over and over to repeat himself, and I felt terrible about it. I felt utterly frustrated and helpless, so I shut my eyes to ask for God's help in understanding Mr. Morris so I could gather his wishes and fulfill them. On top of all this, Mr. Morris's complexion appeared to be growing grayer by the minute.

I offered him a seat and told him I was going to pull his file. As soon as I got into the hall, I took in a few deep breaths. "Please, God," I prayed, "please help me to understand this man. Please get us both through this because, as you can see, he's fading fast."

When I returned to the arrangements office, I found an envelope full of money on the desk. Mr. Morris said, "I don't have long to live. I want to spare my daughter from having to make all these decisions for me. She has a two-week-old baby. She has enough on her plate."

I nodded my head. Reading through his file, I found that Mr. Morris had paid for most of his arrangements about five years prior, except for his memorial plaque and his funeral. I told him what was in the file, and he shook his head that that was correct.

I handed him a catalog of sample memorials, and within moments, he pointed to a flat blue-bronze memorial then to an emblem of a tractor. "I've been a farmer all my life," was what I thought he said.

I then handed him a casket catalog. After looking through about ten pages, Mr. Morris pointed to a maple-wood casket with a light-blue interior. I showed him some panels that could be placed inside the casket lid, explaining that we wanted something that represented his life. He then pointed to a farmer kneeling beside his wheat field. With great clarity, he said, "That's me, and I want to wear my bib overalls, no suits."

I asked about songs and flowers. His response was, "Just have my daughter sing 'How Great Thou Art.' No flowers."

I made the notations and handed him a pen. He placed a big black X at the bottom of the contract. Mr. Morris gathered up my business card and his paperwork. I helped him rise from his chair. He tried to say, "Thank you," as he slowly walked out the door.

Two weeks later, a young mother with a baby in her arms walked into the office, asking to speak with me. "Harlan Morris was my father," she said.

"He took care of his arrangements before he passed," I said.

She looked bewildered. "This whole thing is so strange," she said, shifting her baby in her arms. "I don't even know how my father was physically able to come here." She paused, looking around the room as if the answers she was seeking were written on the walls. "My father has been on hospice for months, and most days, he didn't even have the strength to get out of bed. There were days he was so weak that he couldn't even talk."

Her face was one big question mark. "He hadn't driven in over six months, but he got out of bed to come here?"

"He did," I said.

"What's even more unexplainable," she continued, "is that I would have picked out the exact same things that my father did."

"Your father did what all parents try to do," I reassured. "He wanted to save you from more hurt and confusion. His exact comment to me was, 'She has so much on her plate right now.' I think he thought this was the last thing he could do for you, and he did it because of love."

FUNERAL DIRECTORS CARE

People oftentimes never even consider the importance of the funeral director. Funeral directors go through a two- to-four-year mortuary arts and science training program and are required to complete an apprenticeship ranging from one to three years. They study embalming, restorative art, anatomy, chemistry, microbiology, pathology. In addition to these hard sciences, they're also trained in funeral service planning and funeral counseling. A funeral director is the cornerstone of the deathcare industry.

As if all this isn't enough, a funeral director never knows who or what situation will present itself at any given moment, nor do they know what they'll be required to do until called upon to do it. The general public has no idea of the depth of work and skill involved in trying to get the deceased to look like they're sleeping, instead of depicting the trauma inflicted on the body through pain, accidental injury, or in this case, suicide.

A deeply depressed father of an eighteen-year-old daughter had shot himself in the face, literally taking off his entire face. Compounding this devastating horror was the fact that his daughter was the one who found him.

When Amber came in to make her father's funeral arrangements, she was distraught beyond anything I had seen in all my years working in the deathcare field. Amber was an only child and the only living relative of the deceased. With her that day was her best friend Suzanne and her best friend's mother, June. All three were in a state of frozen shock. Amber would answer a question then break down crying. As soon as her tears eased off just a little, she kept repeating, "His whole face was gone. His whole face was gone."

I felt completely powerless to console this girl in any way. In fact, the longer she was there, the more emotional I felt. Feelings of sorrow, feelings of anger, feelings of disgust for this man who would do this to his own daughter flooded my heart and mind. I wanted to be able to take away her pain and wondered if she would ever be all right after what she witnessed.

The funeral director wrote up all the paperwork and told Amber he would need a recent picture of her father. He also informed her that it would take an extra two days before we could do the funeral service. He ever so gently told her that she was going to need counseling in order to get on with her life. Showing compassion so deep it brought a tear to my eye, he said, "Amber, your dad was a very sick man. Mental illness is just as real as cancer. Don't ever forget that."

After they left, the funeral director asked if I could stay for a while in case someone came in. I nodded that I would because I was afraid that I would break down sobbing if I opened my mouth. "I'm going for a long run, a cold beer, a hot shower, a steak, and to bed—in that order," he said. "It's going to be a long next four days."

As soon as the door closed behind him, I grabbed the box of tissues and let the tears flow. It seemed like they'd never stop. Then I turned the music system on and sang along with every Christian song filling the air.

Four days later, Amber came back in, this time accompanied by an aunt, a cousin, and her best friend. It was thirty minutes before calling hours were to begin. With her people on either side, Amber walked slowly, haltingly, over to the gray metal casket she'd picked out for her father. The funeral director was waiting for her there. There lying in the casket was her father with his face completely reconstructed.

Amber faltered a bit. Her aunt, cousin, and best friend supported her. Gigantic tears flowed out of her eyes, down her cheeks, and off her chin, wetting the top of her blouse. "How...how did you do this?" she stammered. "Why did you do this for me?"

"I reconstructed your father's face inch by inch using a whole lot of sealing agent," the funeral director replied. Amber's and the funeral director's eyes met in a dance of gratitude and compassion. "I wanted you to remember how your father was your whole life, not how sick he was in that one moment in time."

AFTERWORD

Life After the Cemetery

After working at the cemetery/funeral home for over twelve years, I found myself dreading to go to work. The business had been sold to a large corporation, and my job quickly turned into a sales job instead of a position of caring and serving. I then went to work for a small funeral home writing up preneed funerals and helping wherever I was needed.

I stayed there a little over two years. My husband, Joe, retired, and so did I. Two years into retirement, Joe became ill with a rare autoimmune disease, which left him completely paralyzed. I then became a full-time caregiver.

After two years of intense physical therapy, both in a rehabilitation facility and at home, a bout of pneumonia revealed Joe's stage 3 lung cancer. Because of his autoimmune disease, surgery was not an option.

Over the following five years and several more bouts of pneumonia, we made weekly trips to doctors, testing sites, the hospital for blood plasmapheresis, chemotherapy, and radiation. Many times over those years, I sat in the hospital waiting room with Joe, wondering if he would pull through, wondering, "Would I be able to watch his casket being lowered into the vault, to watch the dirt fill his grave? Would I be able to tolerate seeing the sod placed over his grave, hiding the fact that he ever existed? Would I be able to comfort our children?"

Over all those years working in the deathcare industry, I had witnessed between 1,200 to 1,400 burials. At each burial, I prayed, "Eternal rest grant unto them, oh Lord. Let perpetual light shine upon them and may they rest in peace." After about a year of saying this prayer, I realized that a deep feeling of peace would come over me every time I did.

As I walked to my car to head back to the office to turn in the paperwork from the funeral home, the words "all is well" filled my mind and heart. A person's religion didn't matter. Neither did their race, gender, ethnicity, or whether they were rich or poor. "All is well" is what I felt and thought, and that was all I needed to know.

While standing at Joe's grave site almost eight years after the diagnosis of his autoimmune disease, watching his casket being lowered into the vault and the earth shoveled into his grave, I once again heard the words, "All is well."

I shut my eyes to say, "Thank you."

This time, I heard the words, "Love abounds."

There were no more tears left to cry. I had already used them all up in a methodical daily drip watching the cancer slowly take over Joe's body and witnessing his struggle to breathe. There were days I felt deeply lonely, days of anger, days of not wanting to get out of bed, days of feeling it should have been me, days of feeling numb no matter how many people were around, days of tears streaming down my cheeks for no apparent reason while talking to a friend.

Many nights, I was awakened to find my husband's spirit standing at the foot of our bed. Other nights, I'd awaken to feel him tapping on my shoulder, just like he did in life, but I saw no one. On those occasions, I would say, "Go to the light, Joe. Thank you for your love. I'm okay." Then I would be awake the rest of the night.

When COVID came on the scene in March 2020, I found myself watching lots of ministers and life mastery coaches on television, one of whom was Mary Morrissey. "We are spiritual beings having a human experience, not human beings having a spiritual experience," she said one day.

That statement answered so many questions for me. I finally understood. If I am a child of the Almighty and I was created in his image and likeness and he is love, then I must be spirit. I realized that even though my body may decay in the ground, my spirit will always remain because love abounds, and spirit never dies.

Over the lockdown, I started cleaning out my desk. I found many obituaries I had saved, along with notes of gratitude from some of the families I had served. I was reminded of what I had learned years prior: every life has a story, and that story goes beyond death. Our stories need to be told because that's how we make sense of life and, in some cases, death. And so was birthed the book you hold in your hands right now.

Our world has suffered a lot of loss in the last few years. I found this poem by Henry Scott-Holland written in 1910. I pray it helps bring you peace.

"Death Is Nothing at All"

Death is nothing at all.
It does not count.
I have only slipped into the next room.
Nothing has happened.
Everything remains exactly as it was.
I am I, and you are you,
and the old life that we lived so fondly
together is untouched, unchanged.
Whatever we were to each other, that we are still.
Call me by the old familiar name.
Speak of me in the easy way which you always used.
Put no difference into your tone.
Wear no forced air of solemnity or sorrow.
Laugh as we always laughed at the little
jokes that we enjoyed together.
Play, smile, think of me, pray for me.
Let my name be ever the household word that it always was.
Let it be spoken without an effort, without
the ghost of a shadow upon it.
Life means all that it ever meant.

It is the same as it ever was.
There is absolute and unspoken continuity.
What is death but a negligible accident?
Why should I be out of mind because I am out of sight?
I am but waiting for you, for an interval,
Somewhere very near,
Just around the corner.
All is well.
Nothing is hurt; nothing is lost.
One brief moment and all will be as it was before.
How we shall laugh at the trouble of parting when we
meet again!

ABOUT THE AUTHOR

Sandra K. Doyle was born in the Midwest in 1946. Friends and family call her Sandy.

Sandy was married over fifty years and has been blessed with seven children, nineteen grandchildren, and six great grandchildren. Sandy has belonged to the Optimist organization for over twenty years. In 2017 to 2018, Sandy served as governor for Indiana North District Optimists.

Sandy worked in the deathcare industry for over fourteen years, and every day, she would say, "One of these days, I am going to write a book." Today, these words became real.

Printed in the USA
CPSIA information can be obtained
at www.ICGtesting.com
LVHW040737131023
760664LV00002B/233

9 798886 446609